MIDWAY IN MY SONG

Lotte Lehmann.

Midway in My Song

•

THE AUTOBIOGRAPHY
OF
Lotte Lehmann

•

GREENWOOD PRESS, PUBLISHERS
WESTPORT, CONNECTICUT

Originally published in 1938
by The Bobbs-Merrill Company, Indianapolis, Indiana

Reprinted from an original copy in the
collections of the Brooklyn Public Library

First Greenwood Reprinting 1970

Library of Congress Catalogue Card Number 70-109765

SBN 8371-4255-5

Printed in the United States of America

FOREWORD

PERHAPS it is too early to write my memoirs. Perhaps one shouldn't write memoirs before one is ready to forsake the "well-trod stage" that represents the world. But my life has been such a rich one. If you walk through the world with open eyes, and especially if that world is such a one as my world, a world where fascinating travel, and the meeting of interesting people are an almost daily occurrence—you cannot help but get an overflowing stream of impressions and emotions.

This stream of my impressions has formed itself into my book. But just because the stream is so full I find it difficult to mark its borders and keep the flow orderly. Is it possible to interpret fully in one little book a whole lifetime of wonderful and miraculous experiences? Will not a vital emotion—an incident which, when it happened, made you tremble—be missing?

I have tried honestly to be honest. I have tried to relate my life from the cool heights of objectivity. But I must confess that there are many things that I have put away in the storehouse of my thoughts because I feel that they are meant only for me, not for the critical world at large. Those are not facts or happenings. They are insubstantial, almost unreal things that one can only say in verse. Only poetry could be the right expression for them.

There are also many names I have not mentioned. I have not described, for instance, the time I spent in America as fully as my previous career in Europe. Some fine singers, some great conductors with whom I have "made music" are not named. I have spoken only of those who had a deciding influence on my artistic career and growth. I think it would have made the book too voluminous to mention all with whom I have shared the thrill of music. So I would like to use this foreword to say "thank you" to all—all of you who live in my memory. I ask you to understand that it is not lack of love or lack of friendship which prompted me not to include your names in these pages.

"Midway in My Song." This book represents to me a restful pause for breath—a looking back into the valley. I want to go on. Ahead of me I know lies still a goodly climb.

I am now so much one with my art that I could not imagine my life without it. I shall continue to work for music even if time forces me to retire and make a place for youth, youth which will win in the future what to me still is present. I am too serious a servant of my art not to step back *happily* and *willingly,* when that time comes. Even then there will be much for me to do. I shall communicate my impressions to those who want to learn. I can think of no better profession than teaching—a teaching with enthusiasm. It is impossible to create any true work of art without enthusiasm. Perhaps my book can already help those who want to learn. I have experienced so many disappointments—perhaps reading about them will give the student new courage.

If the book can serve youth, if it can be a sign-post to any young one who travels on the road of art, then its purpose will be fulfilled. Believe me, it was not meant to be a document of vanity; it was meant to be a greeting to those who will come and be victorious.

LOTTE LEHMANN.

POSTSCRIPT
MAY, 1938

THIS book of my memoirs was written before Germany annexed Austria.

My blood is German, my whole being is rooted in the German soil. But my conception of art is different from that of my country.

I cannot serve politics. I can only serve that which always has been and still is the mission of my life. I cannot paint political boundaries on the measureless ways of the art-world. I will not, and cannot probe whether the people to whom I give my art are good or bad, believers or unbelievers; nor does it interest me to what race they belong, or to what politics they subscribe. I want to be an artist—nothing else. I want to live in my world which is more beautiful and loftier than all man-made countries or all states, my world of music. I want to sing the songs that I love, without questioning to what race the composer belonged. God put music into my heart and a voice into my throat. I serve Him when I serve music. I no longer understand the land of my birth.

And I who was born a German, and who was bound to Austria with the bonds of deepest love—I stand now at the door of America. I want to become an American citizen. I am sure that I shall find my third home here and that I shall not again need to wander. I want to become a good American. But that which was my beloved Homeland will live on for me in my songs.

LOTTE LEHMANN.

LIST OF ILLUSTRATIONS

FACING
PAGE

Lotte Lehmann . . . . . . *Frontispiece*

My Mother in Her Youth 6

My Father as a Young Man 6

The House in Perleberg Where I Lived in My Childhood 18

As a Little Girl with My Parents and Brother in Perleberg 32

My Parents in Westerland 52

As Sieglinde in *Die Walküre* 70

As the Marschallin in Strauss's *Rosenkavalier* . . . 98

In Title Role of *Fidelio* 122

As Elsa in *Lohengrin* 122

An Early Picture as the Young Composer in *Ariadne auf Naxos*, My First Important Success 148

My Husband 158

In Westerland 166

My Country House in Hinterbrühl, near Vienna . . 178

Lotte Lehmann and Bruno Walter Take a Bow after Their Joint Lieder Recital 192

Lotte Lehmann, Lauritz Melchior and Mrs. Melchior . 212

First Concert with Toscanini 226

Arrival in Sydney 238

LIST OF ILLUSTRATIONS

Lord Leicester

Monmouth in the Tower

My Father and Mother

The Dutch Ambassador, William Joyce Greenhood

And with My Friends at Monmouth Geology

An Interior Stage Coach

An Interior in a House

Astor House in its Early Days

Old Trinity Parish Row

Liberty Place, 1848

A Short Time in the Young Crowd of Printing and Binding, My First Apprentice Shop

Jim Gordon

My Workshop

My Father Killed at Headquarters at Vicksburg

Tom Thumb and Minnie Warren Dwarfs

Buffalo Bill's Wild West

Old Liberty Street, New York

The Lincoln

MIDWAY IN MY SONG

CHAPTER
ONE

EVEN today, I believe, the little local train from Wittenberge, the "clanker" as we children used to call it, still runs clanging through the sparse pinewoods of sandy Priegnitz into the friendly little town of Perleberg where I was born. My mother often used to tell me that the day I was born the snow lay on the ground the height of a man, and the little garden she looked out on from her childbed had become a white frozen fairyland. I have absolutely no recollection of this house. While I was still quite little, my parents moved into the so-called "Ritterschaftshaus," the official residence next to the big Ritterschaft* offices where my father was secretary. We had the whole house to ourselves with a pretty front garden, a big one at the back and a poultry yard. The broad path that led to our playground my parents proudly called the "park." I believe that this "park" is one of my earliest recollections. I can see it now, sunlit and sparkling, bordered with flowers and bushes and trees. There was one

---

* The Ritterschaft is a kind of benevolent society, with branches in various parts of Germany. [Tr.]

part where lilies of the valley—hundreds of them—grew among the bushes. We were not allowed to pick them— father cherished every flower in his garden.

Yet one day is clear in my memory: my mother stood at the end of the pathway—she stretched out her arms to me and I ran through the sunlight to her shouting with joy: "It is spring. . . ." Even today my conception of spring is still bound up with this experience of childhood.

And there never is an Easter when I do not recollect how eagerly we used to hunt for Easter eggs in the park! They were hidden in the slipped boxtrees, in the lily-of-the-valley bed, they hung from the bushes; lovely colored sugar eggs, shiny chocolate ones and hens' eggs dyed bright colors. At the end there was a fair division of spoils between my brother Fritz and myself by which we each got half—all the same it was wonderful to have won and to have really found more than the other. . . .

Fritz was a very wild boy and gave my parents a great deal of trouble by playing truant and with his bad reports and boyish pranks. I always looked up to him with shy admiration. He was gifted and imaginative and even as a boy went his own way. Brimming over with wild spirits, he was always the ringleader of a rather terrifying band of schoolboys who satisfied their lust for action by breaking windowpanes and frightening harmless pedestrians in the town park. Fritz was the grim enemy of my beloved dolls with whom, like the quiet and docile child that I was, I would play for hours; he would

2

pretend he was a bloodthirsty red Indian, and would mercilessly scalp my poor children, paint their fuzzy blonde wigs
red and proudly hang the scalps all dripping with blood from
his belt, unmoved by my piteous tears. It always gave me a
horrid fright when the boys rushed wildly through the park,
and yet in my heart I yearned enviously after them, sad that
I was only a silly little girl who could take no part in their
mad chase, for of course they would have considered it be-
neath their dignity to play with me.

It was lovely, too, when we had visitors, a rare event as our
mother preferred a very retired life and lived only for her
children. Fritz would be summoned to the "best room" where
he had to sing to them. He would stand there, pretty angry at
having to show off, among the red plush furniture under the
large, to me incredibly elegant, spray of dried grasses and
would sing away in his lovely clear boy's voice. His voice was
so sweet and beautiful that everyone prophesied a future for
him as a singer. But unfortunately the school singing teacher
was injudicious enough to let him go on singing a mixture of
soprano, tenor and bass in the choir while his voice was breaking until his lovely voice was gone.

But at that time it seemed full of promise for the future,
whereas my little pipe, as yet quite unnoticed, was employed
only for dolls' lullabies.

My father was a member of the Perleberg Choral Union
which Fritz—very unjustly—had christened "the half lung."
Father had a pleasing tenor and sang with gusto, practicing his

3

parts furiously like a true official. His sister, Tante Lenchen, a poor deformed creature, sickly and embittered, who died young, is said to have had the voice of an angel. She lived in Prenzlau, the home town of both my parents, and used to send us lovely toys on every festive occasion. She had knitted our "Kobold" with her own hands. Kobold was the most original doll I ever had. He was entirely made of different-colored wools. Today he would be labeled "arts and crafts"; at that time everyone thought he was mad—except us children. I loved the long, thin, wobbly, woolly man passionately, and his pink knitted face with the black button eyes seemed beautiful to me. But strange what impulses of cruelty there are in a child's soul; I remember exactly how Fritz once condemned poor Kobold to death. He strung him up on the door of the coal house in the yard and we pelted him with snowballs until he was dripping wet. To this day I am ashamed of how exultantly I took part in this attempted murder. But as he hung there, a poor wet bundle, we suddenly fell silent, shamefacedly took him down and laid him on the warm kitchen hearth. There he lay drying beside our tom Maunzi who, with an indignant look, had already resigned his rightful place in favor of this newcomer. I wonder where you are now, dear little Kobold! How I wish I could see once again your stupid little pink woolly face, which had so much more personality than any of the dolls with the stiff wax cheeks whose flaxen locks I so carefully combed

4

every night while you, very dear yet slightly despised, lay flung in a corner somewhere!

Ah, how these memories of childhood crowd back on me! I can still hear the song of Zimmermann the night watchman in the quiet streets: "Hear ye people what I say . . . ," the daily ringing of Peter the milkman's bell, and the shrill whistle of my special friend the ragman. For me that was an electrifying signal! I used to beg Mother for a few rags—simply anything! And, even if sometimes I only managed to wheedle a tattered old stocking out of her, what a shining prize beckoned to me. From an unspeakably filthy hiding place in his cart the ragman would pull out a grisly object the mere thought of which today makes me feel sick—St. John's bread. It was old, hard as stone, sickly sweet and tasted and smelt of the rags it had lain under; but for us children it was the greatest delicacy. . . . It tasted almost as good as the dreadful sirupy raspberry juice at the yearly shooting match in the town park which to us was about the greatest treat of all in the way of noise and excitement. And Frau Braun, the butter woman from the neighboring village of Duepow, shared our opinion. Her son and his friends used to drink this delicious beverage even with smoked eel. . . .

How lovely too were those clear bright autumn days when Fritz took me with him to the wide stubble fields and we released the gaily colored kites which we had glued together in the evenings under Father's supervision: laughing yellow

5

sun-faces, terrible devils' ones with long paper tails and tassels dangling like fantastic earrings. And when the bold flier finally descended again from dizzy heights and lay beside us, a good little toy with its bright paper face turned skyward, we would crouch blissfully round a blazing bonfire. Any old withered rubbish that we found in the stubble was stacked up and set fire to. It was a point of honor to regard the potatoes baked in the flames as a great delicacy and to find them marvelous, and I chewed away bravely at the horrid smoky things and made enormous efforts to share the delight of my brother who devoured them rapturously. . . .

For one year we also had our grandparents staying with us, my father's parents, simple old people. Grandmother, who was thin and not very amiable, did not get on very well with Mamma; there were frequent tears which made me very nearly hate her; for nothing was so terrible to me as to see my dear mother crying. An accident had made Grandfather slightly weak-minded. We were very fond of him and nearly died laughing when we found him in the depths of winter on a snowy bench in the park looking with astonishment at our anxious faces and explaining with a good-humored smile: "I just wanted to hear the nightingales sing. . . ." He never grasped the fact that he was with his eldest son in Perleberg. He always thought he was in his native town Frankfurt-on-the-Oder, and he would often stand at the window in deepest meditation amazed at this new street in Frankfurt. And when I said: "But, Grandfather, you're in Perleberg!" he would

6

My Father as a Young Man.

My Mother in Her Youth.

look at me with profound surprise, shake his white head on which a little black velvet cap embroidered with elegant garlands of flowers was invariably perched, and murmur contentedly: "Well, and quite nice too." He died "nicely" and peacefully and with childlike unawareness while staying with his second son in Berlin, without ever realizing that, shortly before, Grandmother had closed her eyes forever. He was always waiting for her, indeed, ever smiling and good-natured though he was, he would get quite angry that she never came home. . . .

I remember him well. He looked rather like the Father Christmas who always used to pay a strictly personal call on us—Mother dressed up in an old suit of Father's and always greeted by us with a poem recited with beating hearts and knocking knees. My eyes always looked for Mother in this hour of need—where was she now when it was so important? "Mother's gone to Roehl the baker's," Father would inform me, which was not very enlightening, for what did she want just then at Roehl the baker's when the Christmas tree was lit and the whole house smelled of delicious homemade cakes? And how was it that Father laughed until he cried and how did he know Father Christmas so well? Still Father Christmas was so very nice and looked at me with such lovely dark warm eyes that I would pluck up courage. And then, when he had gone, Mother would suddenly reappear and we would rush up to her and have to tell her everything. And even Fritz, several years older than I and "in the know," joined in the conspiracy and rejoiced in his little sister's illusions. Then we would sing Christmas hymns and the old tune: *Stille Nacht, heilige Nacht* would be transfigured by my mother's wonderful velvety golden contralto.

But within what narrow limits was that precious voice confined: the deep cello tone of that heavenly organ was swallowed up by the four walls of our "best room," the red plush furniture and the stupid bunch of dried grasses. Lack of understanding on her father's part was to blame for the loss of a voice which should have rejoiced a world. A professor of music who once by chance heard my mother's lovely young voice asked her father for permission to give this voice to the world was abruptly dismissed with the words: "My daughter a singer, my daughter a *comédienne?*"

Mother, according to our standards in those days, came of a fairly "well-to-do" family. She had grown up in a great mill, the *Draussenmuehle* in Prenzlau, in a household where money, so to speak, played no part. But when the robust healthy father unexpectedly died, his large family of young children and their suffering, infinitely kind mother were suddenly left without any means.

After a tender youthful romance which ended in the war of 1870 with the heroic death of her young, still childlike lover, Mother out of warm affection married our dear father, then standing on the threshold of a lengthy official career. So very soon the lovely young wife forgot all about singing when care knocked at the door, and all her tender, affectionate

8

thoughts were for her husband, her first-born, her widowed invalid mother and her destitute brothers and sisters.

My poor ailing grandmother died before I ever saw her. Her ivy-wreathed grave lies in Boizenburg in the Uckermark, and I frequently go there as to a shrine and deck it with flowers, for I know only that she was dear and good and fine, and I often imagine that anything good and fine in my life has come from her who died when I was quite little, and one of whose last joys was my birth. Perhaps her dear soul has been a guardian angel of my life—who knows? I believe it.

We had a great deal of illness in the home. Doctors' and druggists' bills ate up everything. Mother became a permanent victim to a painful nervous gastric trouble—and I would often see her crying bitterly because there was not enough money in the house. Moreover she never felt really at home in Perleberg and longed for her brothers and sisters who all lived in Berlin. Father often applied to be transferred to Berlin where the head office of the Ritterschaft is situated, although he was devoted heart and soul to his beloved garden. So thanks to Providence we were able to spend our early childhood in the freedom of God's nature, in the pleasant humdrum peace of a country town, and not behind high walls and in streets of whirling dust. . . .

CHAPTER
TWO

IN THE meantime I had gone to school and was a proper "high-school girl," learned my lessons dutifully and found friends and playmates. Selma, who is still my dear and faithful friend, used to come round every day and we romped about the garden where Papa had made us a lovely playground with horizontal and parallel bars, swing ropes and a swing. He had also laid out a little garden of my very own which I had to look after myself. Mohr, our good old poodle, was a faithful friend, also Maunzi, the yellow tom. But we always went in fear of his life! Our neighbor, the sheriff of Jagow, later the chief of police in Berlin, had a fierce hatred of all cats because they drove all the singing birds away from his wonderful park. So he mercilessly shot every member of the feline race that trespassed on his grounds. For a long time Maunzi with great cunning eluded his sharp eyes, but at last he met his doom. How I hated that "cat-murderer," how I enjoyed breaking his windows in revenge, egged on by Fritz and Meta, our "maid-of-all-work" who had also a large share in my childish affections.

10

Meta loved telling me blood-curdling tales and must certainly have it on her conscience that all my life I have been afraid to be alone in a dark room or to go along a dark street by myself, for this is the sort of thing that sticks in my memory: "And suddenly the coffin lid rose and the pale Countess Elvira stepped out."

"Oh Heavens, Meta, wasn't she properly dead?"

"No, she was just in a trance. Or perhaps she was dead but you know it was a haunted house. This house is haunted too, Lotte, you can take it from me. Just the other day I saw a gray figure on the stairs. Ask Mamma, ask Tante Lieschen."

Shivers would go down my spine.

Tante Lieschen, Mother's youngest sister who often came to visit us, firmly believed in ghosts. She still swears by all that is holy that the house where I spent my childhood was horribly haunted—and I like to believe her, because it fits in with the romantic charm of that house, overgrown with wild vine, with its green shutters and the yellow gravel paths of the front garden, where thousands of sweet-smelling acacia blossoms danced in the spring wind, tossed down on us from the old tree in front of our windows.

Meanwhile my little fluttering bird's-voice had already become the joy of our singing class. Indeed, when there was to be a school performance of an operetta called *Queen Louise* I was given the solo part of the Queen, although by my age I shouldn't have been allowed even in the choir of the upper school.

11

Proud, unconcerned and unself-conscious as only a child can be, I sang out my part to the crowded hall. This gave rise to a few tentative opinions: "If she goes on singing as well as that you should perhaps have her voice trained. Perhaps she could become a singer. . . ." My parents were very proud but Father thought I should learn something "sensible" and become a teacher—"perhaps even a secondary-school teacher," he added uncertainly—but Mother was all for my being a singer. Perhaps she wanted to see her own unfulfilled dreams realized in her child.

In the meantime I was not concerned about my future: my good behavior at school relaxed, and I began to be a proper tomboy. One of my favorite amusements was letting one of my school friends hang on to my long thick pigtail and swinging her round and round. Or time without number Selma and I would go up to the window of a drunken old scamp, make deep and polite curtseys, and in tones of great respect say, "Good evening, Herr Balke," and then run away giggling. The first time Herr Balke, full of sweet brandy, would reply, deeply flattered; but gradually he would realise that we were making fun of him and after a rapturously received orgy of abuse would go reeling off to Father to complain of those "damned hussies." Father would propitiate him with a small sum of money which he pocketed, raising his hat and calling down blessings on us all, even on me, a contrite sinner. Then off he would go.

Sometimes Father got a bonus in summer and we all went

12

off to Warnemünde on the Baltic. No words can describe
how I suffered those last days before our departure! All
sorts of possible obstacles rose to my mind—could anything
be more likely than that the house, together with all our
traveling cases, should catch fire? But at last there we were
in the train—third class, of course—and I would listen with
rapture to the song of the wheels that really sounded as Meta
had said: "I think I can, I think I can." And, just before the
train arrived: "I knew I could!"

Then Warnemünde—sea air, sea waves, white beach, sun
and wind! And Mother's eyes always laughing, Father contented, and Fritz covered with the medals and badges of his
great position as Kommandant of his proud sand castle!
Naturally we did not live on the sea front in expensive hotels
and villas but in the town, and in the evening I used to stand
and look through the shining windowpanes of the brightly-
lit Kurhaus restaurant and gaze at "the rich." "Hotel food"
was to me the epitome of all the culinary delights in that
unattainable paradise. . . .

On the pier, where the sharp sea wind lashed the shimmering green waves, sat Fritz who sometimes caught the
ghastliest collection of monsters: devilfish, common crabs—
and sometimes even a "normal" fish as well. I kept nervously out of his way, for, from early childhood, the thought
had worried and tormented me that we kill animals to eat
them and we derive pleasure from their suffering. At home
I would always run to the farthest corner of the garden when

13

I knew that a hen was going to be killed, and I remember that at one time I actually hated Meta because I saw her killing a fish. At sight of the convulsively twitching body I rushed out of the kitchen in a panic and hid in the garden— and when at midday I slunk hesitatingly into the house, my first question, trembling and stammering, was, "Is it dead?" Meta went into fits of laughter and showed it to me, all baked a golden-brown, but I looked at her rough, work-coarsened hands with horror, and many evenings passed before I crept back stealthily to the kitchen to shudder over further complicated episodes in the destiny of poor Countess Elvira.

"Oh Meta," I said, "it must be simply wonderful to be a Countess. Let's pretend we are. Let's play Countesses."

Henceforth this became our favorite game. Selma, Meta and I gave ourselves the grandest names, pulled off the bed-covers which Mother had unsuccessfully dyed a ghastly gleaming reddish-lilac and fastened them round our waists as priceless court trains. Then we went mincing about, re-sourcefully inventing aristocratic turns of speech and keeping as near as possible to the wealth of adventures of the Countesses in our novels. Meta herself had a passion for the game, got off work whenever she possibly could to join in, and would fight passionately for some particularly accept-able aristocratic rôle. Naturally she had very little time to play with us and would look after us with a sad face as, in-credibly distinguished and grand, we "swept by" her sink.

For a moment she would pause in her task of washing up the enormous pile of dishes and sniff resignedly: "Oh, you're playing Countesses," but soon we would hear her shrill voice singing happily away again at a soldiers' song, for Meta loved the military. She often told me about them— and soon it seemed to me that soldiers were the only really worth-while people. I shared her deep scorn for "civilians" without actually knowing what a civilian meant. . . .

One day Selma came with the supremely exciting news that her father had met the director of the little traveling theater which was just then giving a few evening performances on the stage of the hotel Zum Deutschen Kaiser. His name was Camillo von Kunzendorff, he played all the chief parts, his wife was leading lady, and he had given us tickets for that evening. Our joy was indescribable! Hitherto we had seen only one play, *Cinderella*, performed by a troupe of midgets. And now we sat among the audience in the greatest excitement. They did some sort of crime play that was nearly as complicated as our Countess-novels—but we felt the glamour of the stage even though it was only the wobbly little stage of the Deutschen Kaiser. . . .

But even more wonderful than seeing the play was having to go round once to Frau von Kunzendorff to give her a parcel. We stood gazing at her in awed admiration. She was a tall, slim woman with interesting features, wild dun-colored hair, tired, resigned eyes and a voice of uncommonly deep timbre, as if it were broken and this curiously dry, un-

15

resonant, harsh voice somehow made a terrific impression on me. She spoke to us very kindly while she sewed huge spangles and glittering jewels on to a robe that to us looked truly regal. Nothing seemed more desirable to me than the life of this tired, harassed, worn-out woman who must have buried many, many dreams before; hung with sorry spangles, she came to play her queen's parts in that deep, breaking voice, the anxious listening expression of the hard-of-hearing in her faded eyes—up there on the stage of the village inn.

And now we began playing "theaters" too. The overgrown summerhouse made a marvelous stage. We chose a comedy where I had to play the part of a young man. A suit of my big brother's hung loosely round me and a huge mustache gave me a manly appearance. We had also real printed theater tickets, as one of the company was the daughter of the owner of a printing press. It was a great evening for us, almost more exciting than my birthday parties which filled our house once a year with swarms of my school friends— the climax of the evening being a polonaise led by Father with fairy lights and lusty choruses.

Altogether a great deal of singing went on at home when Mother wasn't having one of her nervous gastric attacks or crying. Father generally got very cross and grumpy too at such times and I used to flee to the garden to escape the stormy atmosphere. Or I would sit dumbly at table indefatigably painting, on any scrap of paper I could get hold of, pictures of brightly colored dolls, gentle angels with great

16

wings, or better still—Hell. It was just as Father described it to us: the poor souls doomed to roast eternally standing in a huge pot wringing their hands, the Devil poking up the fire and his grandmother chewing merrily away at a freshly cooked human leg. This uncommonly pleasing picture was one I was particularly fond of portraying, and I was deeply hurt if nobody but myself was able to follow the painting in all its details. . . .

But on nice cozy evenings we used to sit round and sing dear old sentimental folk songs. Father's light tenor and our shrill childish voices mingled with the velvety tones of Mother's beautiful contralto which, although she always sang seconds, yet rose and hovered above us all. Then we would be silent for a while and she would go on alone with "On the bridge at Strassburg," "Sleep, my sweet child," and "In a cool glen." And we would join in the chorus, Father imitating the mill wheel in the cool glen by hitting the chair leg with a stick, and Fritz rubbing a big sheet of paper on the ground—to represent the waterfall. The gas would be turned down and only one candle allowed to burn. We were delighted with the atmosphere we created in this way.

For my parents' silver wedding, as a surprise for Father, Mother had let me have piano lessons which she secretly paid for with great difficulty out of housekeeping money. I sat at the piano, nervously swallowing with emotion, and in a voice choked with tears sang something like this: "But Oh, how quickly they had flown those five and twenty year, and now

17

as silver-wedded you again to me appear" (or some such thing). It was not quite clear how my parents, after twenty-five years should "again to me appear" since I was born late in their married life, and that is perhaps why I banged with such energy on the wretched keys of the decrepit old piano and stood as hard as I could on the pedal, to cover up the stupid words and my emotion. . . . Fritz stood rather shamefacedly beside me, for all those secret piano lessons had never managed to make him learn to play the song, "Cuckoo calls out of the wood"; he much preferred rushing into the wood himself and playing truant, so the good old teacher came to Mother and begged her not to waste another penny on such a bad boy. He was delighted, and felt that he was delivered from the necessity of doing any more practicing—not that he had ever done any—but much to their astonishment, he explained to our parents in enthusiastic terms how absolutely necessary for the general education of an ambitious boy it was to have dancing lessons. The grant of this request conjured up such a radiant face that I begged with tears for dancing lessons too. So I was allowed to go to dancing school with him and there I found my first admirer, an honest, sturdy farmer's son in Fritz's class at school. He became my most assiduous partner, gave me chocolate and, the height of all my dreams of longing, a paint box with gleaming water colors—most helpful for the increasingly lurid flames of my hell-fires. But I found it unspeakably silly that he should be "in love" with me, as Fritz very scornfully said.

18

The House in Perleberg Where I Lived in My Childhood.

"Are you in love with your partner too?"

"Which partner?"

"You know, the one you're always dancing with—Alma."

Fritz grew fiery red.

"Oh, that's quite different—you couldn't understand that yet," he said very distantly and visibly perturbed. This was something new to me. I hadn't seen him so embarrassed since the days of school reports. . . . In those days he used to take a long time coming home, and whereas I from afar would beamingly wave my report like a flag of victory, he would take his very reluctantly out of his pocket, muttering something about its not being his fault and unfairness and idiotic teachers. No, school had never plunged him into such confusion as now the pretty blue eyes of Alma, also a "high-school girl" a couple of classes above me with two magnificent thick black plaits and a round little face like milk and roses.

Heaven only knows how he managed to wheedle a couple of shillings out of Mother, and how she, poor thing, could spare them, for at home every shilling counted—but it made a great sensation at school: he had given Alma a ring—"real silver," it was enviously affirmed, but this "real silver" engagement somehow came to nothing. When I told this most interesting and exciting piece of news to our neighbor's son, Fritz Gerloff, he declared solemnly: "I say, we might perhaps get engaged, don't you think? Just give me your hand and now everything is all right, we're engaged."

I gave him my hand, glad to have found a husband so

19

soon, for I knew from Mother that it was bad for a girl to be left "on the shelf." Then we looked at each other, shy and embarrassed, until Fritz burst out: "Oh, it's only a joke. . . ." And in spite of a certain disappointment I was really most relieved to be free of a rather gloomy and irksome obligation. . . .

My first love, when I was twelve, was for our singing teacher Konrad Strey, "Konny," as we all adoringly called him. I stole pencils for him, secretly laid flowers on his desk and in a diary with a key which I begged from Mother I wrote my first verses, full of passionate protestations and longing for death. . . . He married a very beautiful girl who thus earned the passionate hatred of the whole class. But I was very surprised that my heart didn't break, as usually happened in our novels. . . .

Both Selma and Elli, another friend of mine, were already in love's bondage. Two magnificent grammar-school boys had won their hearts. So there were walks in the town park and the woods, and I always trotted dutifully along without any idea that I wasn't really wanted, until one day they brought along a third boy for me. "Perhaps he'll marry you," said practical little Selma. "He's very much in love with you. Girls often marry the love of their youth."

So I went on walks with him and thought anxiously: "Must I marry him?" I didn't like him a bit. He told me about Berlin and Wertheim's enormous shop that was so huge that many people went in in winter only because it was

20

so lovely and warm there. They didn't buy a thing, only wandered through. I didn't believe a single word. Could anyone blame me for not wanting to marry such an awful liar? Who would believe in such big shops? I only knew Tiess's shop in Perleberg; now that was big according to my standards, then there was Fräulein Wilke's toyshop where there were the lovely black dolls which—next to Kobold—had been my favorite toys. No, this Berlin store sounded to me suspiciously like poppycock. I came home very depressed and confessed to Mother with tears about the secret walk. She, the ever-forgiving, forgave this too, and finally said impatiently: "Now stop crying, I'm not angry any more."

Then I threw myself on the sofa in despair and sobbed: "But I can't marry him."

My confirmation came and with it the firm determination to renounce the wickedness of the world and become a nun or a nursing sister at least. None of which prevented me from being very proud of my first long black dress.

Penitently I knelt at the altar and heard the words: "I will bless thee, be thou a blessing."

And God has blessed me. He has given me my voice and my art—and through it the potentiality of giving joy to others, of being, in a sense, a blessing . . . and for this I am thankful.

CHAPTER
THREE

SOON after my confirmation Father was transferred to
Berlin. Mother's dream of many years was at last fulfilled. Full of expectation we left our quiet little home town,
and even father, devoted as he was to his garden, possessed
the gift of taking life easily and looked forward to the city
after years of narrow small-town life. Fritz had gone on
ahead. For Mother's sake, he had given up his dream of
going to sea and owing to lack of money my parents had
long since given up their dream of letting their son study.
So he was to be a clerk. His imaginative young spirit was
confined in a joyless cage of daily routine from which he
could only escape on the wings of his beautiful verses.

I myself had to go on attending school in Berlin, because,
at Father's wish, I was to be a teacher. So I went to the Ulrich
High School which had a teachers' training college attached,
and sat there, a proper little country cousin, among the
Berlin girls who scornfully called me "our Lotte from Perleberg."

I tried as hard as I could to feel "towny," heroically suppressed any longings for the beautiful forsaken paradise of

22

our garden, and overcame my disappointment at my first sight of the Tiergarten (the town park) where instead of animals, as I had expected, I saw cars and electric trains. How I marveled at Unter den Linden, that broad west-end boulevard! But I regarded with a mixture of scorn and sympathy the lime trees which gave the beautiful street its name: miserable, stunted, insignificant—how I longed for the old lime trees in Perleberg—"at home," I thought with a heavy heart. . . .

We lived in the cheap northern quarter of Berlin, in the Hochmeister Strasse. Mother was glad to be with her brothers and sisters, Father regarded it as a kind of promotion that he was now chief Ritterschaft secretary and was very pleased about it. But Fritz went his own mysterious way, wrote poems that he always used to tear up, wore floppy bow ties and a huge wide-brimmed hat and was blissfully happy to think that he "looked like an artist." With a few colleagues he started a club which boasted the proud name of "Justitia" and some sort of idealistic aims. The principal business was a great deal of beer-drinking. . . .

Before very long I had found some very good friends at school. Our class mistress, Fräulein Vogel, shared the fate of many young teachers: she was passionately adored. She was very pretty and nice and I believe that even I won her motherly heart. I brought her my poems and stories and how proud and happy I was at her praise! She often said: "You'll certainly be a great writer one day."

23

The hour when we got back our essays was always the one in the week which almost everybody feared! But I looked forward happily to it, glad to hear certain praise—whereas in every other subject I was decidedly below the average. And so it happened that our headmaster, Ulrich, who, as we advanced to the highest form, was our form-master, refused to believe that I had written my essays myself. He knew me only from his own personal experience of me in the mathematics class—and there, even at the simplest question I presented a picture of misery. . . .

I waited in excitement for the headmaster's verdict when he handed back our first piece of homework. Below my essay stood clear and distinct: "Judging from the accomplishments hitherto displayed in school I doubt the authenticity of this work." A suppressed cry of indignation went through the whole class. I stood up, flaming with resentment, and asked to be allowed immediately to write a new essay under my unjust accuser's eyes. Ulrich—secretly known as Ulli—had a keen sense of humor. He regarded with amusement the general insurrection and said: "Very well, noble poetess, sit down and write what you like—write about Christmas. You can give your imagination free play."

I did—and was gloriously rehabilitated. . . .

From now on Ulli was "my passion," as the adored one was secretly called. So unbounded was my enthusiasm for him that the whole form was infected and a regular "Ulli-complex" broke out. We worked like mad for him, lived only

24

for the hours when he taught us, were rapturous at a word of praise and suicidal at a reproof. Once in the literature lesson when we were doing the *Koenigsleutnant,* each reading a part, I was given the part of young Goethe, and when Ulli, smiling craftily, said: "But for this part you must be very much in love—do you think you can manage that?" the entire class burst into a peal of laughter and yelled assent. Then I began to read, and every enamored word that young Goethe had to say I addressed to him while he looked out of the window, smiling heedlessly. He was a wonderful teacher and I still recollect with gratitude his instructive and enthralling lectures which we followed breathlessly, ignorant flappers suddenly become eager students at his words. Time and again he would say to us: "Go your own ways, don't trot after the herd. Be personalities. Become what you are, that is the best thing in life. . . ."

In this rich and unforgettable last year at school occurred another charming experience. Fritz and his friend Erich, who lived for a time with us as a boarder—he was the son of a country teacher and his parents wanted him to be well protected in "that sink of iniquity, Berlin"—had discovered two nice pretty girls in the neighborhood. They were sisters of eighteen and nineteen who had also not failed to notice their adoring admirers opposite. So a kind of signaling game started on both sides. There was always something that needed polishing at the window or the plants to be watered or pruned, even though the good fat mother often appeared with threatening mien and put an end to the dumb conversations by violently drawing the curtains. Else and Trude were their names, as the boys Fritz and Erich soon found out. Else was going away shortly to be a children's nurse in the Tiergarten district, so Fritz told us gloomily, but Trude was staying, Erich added brightly. There was also a brother, a student of philology, and a little sister. I had frequently seen the student also at the window, he was my brother's age and I thought he looked very nice. He had often smiled across at me, which filled me with pride and dread, and I sometimes thought that the glow of his cigarette in the evening at the window was meant as a greeting to me. And when one day the mother opposite came across to our mother and requested her to tell her son and his friend to stop this perpetual staring across because her daughters were "nice girls"—my secret fears were not for the boys alone. . . . But my anxiety was superfluous: the two mothers parted with mutual assurances of good will—and arrangements were made for a joint family outing on Sunday to the *Pankgrafen,* an inn popular with excursionists, with a band in the garden. The band was said to have a simply fascinating conductor who gave a marvelous rendering of the famous song about the glimmering glowworms. . . . Even if he had played a funeral march we young things would have listened with the same enthusiasm! We quickly made friends and paired off under our parents' eyes, the mothers' benevolent, the fathers'

26

reflectively consenting, Fritz and Else, Erich and Trude, and Willy and I. We were all still just half grown-up, our parents saw us getting engaged at some not too distant date and placidly contemplated this peaceful solution of one of the most difficult of future problems. None of us had wealth or property, but we were all unpretentious and demanded nothing of the future that it didn't seem prepared to offer us. And wasn't that a great deal for hearts so young and ready for happiness?

They were wonderful—those outings! We used to meet down below on the street—Frau Hilke always good-natured, on her arm the plush knitting bag that seemed to have come into the world with her, for she was never seen without it.

Old Hilke, silent and slightly irritable, would join up with Father, and they both talked politics. This was also a standard feature of the Sunday program. They talked politics by the hour, although it really must have been rather difficult and unproductive, as they were both staunch Conservatives with the same opinions. But there must be a great fascination in hearing your own opinion corroborated, "underlined and ratified" so to speak . . . in any case they both derived a great deal of satisfaction from it. Father spoke and Father Hilke nodded his approval. Now and again Father tried in vain to challenge him with a: "Perhaps you don't think so?"

But the answer was invariably a loyal and deliberate: "Oh yes I do."

27

Then a resigned sigh from Father who would have much preferred a violent argument. . . .

Ah, they were wonderful—those Sunday outings!

Getting a place on the crowded trams first of all—that in itself was a pleasure! What did it matter if you were half dragged along hanging on to the step in a frightful crush—there were strong arms to hold you tight and that was nicest of all. . . . In the Pankgrafen we generally found a free table near the band. Mother Hilke had a passion for hearing the trumpets and drums from very near—and the cornet solo "Good night, my darling child" always moved her to tears. . . .

So to the accompaniment of music we consumed the cakes we had brought with us and drank Berlin coffee. From the bottomless depths of her knitting bag Frau Hilke would bring out a magnificent collection of cakes and sandwiches. Her merry little eyes twinkled at us when Erich became unreasonably jealous again and imagined that his Trude had smiled at the fascinating glowworm-conductor, or when Fritz, an aesthete from top to toe, begged his Else, in the name of beauty, never again to eat a cheese sandwich, to which she answered: "Nonsense!"

Fritz grew pale.

In that moment he broke it off with Else for the nine hundred and ninety-ninth time. . . .

Finally!

In her he saw his ideal, remote as a star, and so he tyran-

28

nized terribly over the poor child whom he never called anything but his queen. They often quarreled and always made it up just when the general parental head-shaking threatened to turn to philosophic discourses: warnings against getting married if you couldn't agree when you were engaged, when it wasn't even a "proper" engagement with a ring and a party. . . . But Fritz and Else would be laughing again—and he would see her home by secret paths through the Tiergarten where she was governess in a fine house; and when he came home late at night he would write her letters as thick as books in which he probably informed her of everything he had forgotten to tell her. . . . At all events Erich told me that one night he had awakened out of lovely dreams to see Fritz sitting at the writing desk in his hat and coat.

"He was writing," said Erich, "as if his life depended on it. I asked him quite bewildered how late it was and Fritz growled: 'Five o'clock!' Then I said: 'What are you doing, man?' and do you know what he said—quite quietly, as if it were the most natural thing in the world: 'I'm writing to my queen. . . .' "

This story would then be repeated and laughed over hundreds of times. Fritz would look round the whole table with a pitying smile. But the little scornful expression round Else's mouth which she brought back to the humble north from the aristocratic neighborhood of the Tiergarten, would deepen. . . .

Erich, however, used to discuss solidly and reasonably the prospects of their future marriage with his Trude, and her charming blonde mop nodded happy agreement to everything.

Willy too had, with his first kisses, confessed his love for me on the dark way home from the Pankgrafen, and said he had really meant to wait until I had left school before he told me, so as not to disturb me in my schoolwork. (Oh dear—I let him keep the lovely delusion that I was a good hardworking girl, whereas I now worked exclusively for Ulli, my ideal—and even that was weakening considerably in the proximity of vivid reality. . . .) But I knew anyway that he was fond of me, and he might as well say it now. I thought so too and entirely agreed with him. . . .

So the last short weeks of my school days flew by like a dream. At my urgent request Father had given up the idea of having me trained as a teacher. For, apart from the fact that in many subjects I was really atrociously bad and would have great difficulty in ever getting through an examination, I had also seen with horror the terrible agonies of the poor young pupil teachers when they had to take "test classes." Before the sharp and often pitiless eyes of the staff, before the ready mockery of Ulli's smile, they had to stand at the desk with knocking knees and teach us. They were delivered into our hands, for we with childish cruelty would frequently give a wrong answer on purpose and so join in a little unauthorized "testing" ourselves, instead of trying to help the poor girls by being doubly attentive. But we always considered it rather a disgrace to be taught by people about our own age. At sixteen we considered ourselves quite grown-up! So in agitated words I explained my absolute inability to exhibit myself in front of so many eyes—and anyway I was soon going to be married.

"What do you mean by soon?" asked Father, wrinkling up his forehead. "Just now Willy has one year's service to do—"

"Yes, with the Cockchafer* Regiment of the Guards," I interrupted with proud emphasis. . . .

"All right, with the Cockchafers—I know. I also know that the Cockchafer uniform is very becoming, but that doesn't answer my question."

Father was a real official and didn't like being sidetracked. "Well, when he has done his year's service he will first have to go on with his studies, then take his examination and so on. But in the meantime you must be earning money. I shall send you to a commercial school and then I hope you will get a good post in the Ritterschaft. Perhaps later you'll be able to get into the head office as a secretary. You'd get a pension there too."

"What do I want with a pension? I'm going to marry Willy, Papa."

Papa made no answer. He looked meditatively before him and said: "For we can't do anything about singing. I

---

* "Maikäfer" (—Cockchafer) is a nickname given to one of the regiments of the Guard. [Tr.]

31

haven't the money to have you trained. And who knows whether you'd come to anything. But here in the Ritterschaft you're sure of your bread and butter."

I said yes and amen. What did I care about it all: we had lots to do at school—a great farewell party to mark the close of our school days. We had to make a collection to give Ulli a silver goblet in memory of us all, as we had all adored him without exception. Selma, my childhood friend from Perleberg, came to stay with us, met a friend of my brother's called Ernst Betz, who was already in a good position with prospects, and managed to get engaged to him before we had recovered from our astonishment. (They both live in Berlin; we are very good friends, and their only daughter Lotti is my dear little godchild, a sweet creature with Selma's cheeky snub nose.)

When I left school we meant to move to Grosslichterfelde, a pretty suburb of Berlin, so that Mother could have better air. She was in very poor health—and, although she never admitted it, she often longed in summer for the lovely Perleberg garden. So father had rented a nice flat in a simple villa in Lichtenfelde—we had even the use of the garden—how his eyes shone!

Our school party came in the middle of our preparations for removal. We had had ourselves photographed with Ulli, and, visibly moved, he had accepted the wreathed goblet although he scolded us a little for giving him a present; then he said to us: "Children, you were nicest when you were

As a Little Girl with My Parents and Brother in Perleberg.

up to your silly tricks. I think model children are awful. Not that you were that by any means—at least, so my teachers say. With me you were just putting it on! So don't become model grownups. Go your own ways! And forget about school and all that nonsense. Life lies before you—live it! And one other thing: don't tell any of the other girls here what I've told you, do you understand?"

Such was Ulli's farewell. As he shook hands with me and I with a childish half-curtsey stammered a tearful word of thanks, I thought my heart would break. In spite of Willy. . . . In the afternoon there were coffee and cakes— donated by various mothers—but Ulrich, whom we had invited, didn't come. He thought it was an "awful" idea and laughingly declined. . . . So now we were just our- selves . . . and we were overcome by sentimental emotion. The air was filled with protestations of eternal friendship! I made an impassioned speech which ended with a general uproar of cheering and sobbing "three cheers for our beloved, unforgettable and highly honored Ulli." We fell weeping into one another's arms, and later I heard that the porter, a good, real old Berliner, had said: "No, I've never seen any- thing so barmy in all my life. Instead of the lasses being glad that they were leaving the silly old school, there they were howling away like dogs and yelling three cheers for Ulli! That's what happens when you wear patent-leather shoes and put grease on your hair—girls like that. What will they come to?" So sadly misunderstood was our great love.

CHAPTER
FOUR

IT WAS really very hard to leave the Hochmeister Strasse. The neighboring windows beckoned in such a friendly way, although things were no longer going so well. Fritz and Else were having "rows" with each other more frequently, the periods of mutual understanding became fewer, and finally they said straight out that they didn't suit each other and so it would be better to break it off. And in reply to my indignant protests Erich murmured that one shouldn't get tied up—that they also were still too young—leaving me speechless at this change of feelings. "Thank goodness Willy and I don't think we are too young," said I, the youngest of them all, and flounced indignantly out of the room. . . .

But of course moving into the new house and no more "having to go to school" were exciting events that made the grief of parting recede into the background. I helped Mother energetically in the house—we had only a woman to do the heaviest work—so I had to help quite a lot. But it was fun running around the new house in a blue apron, armed with broom and duster. Only often I would look at the clock and think: "Eleven o'clock—literature. Oh Ulli, I wonder what you are talking about today!"

But then I would immediately think of his words: "Life lies before you—live it!" and I would work on, singing. All day long my voice rang through the house, and all my songs were joyful greetings to Willy. He was coming to visit us now as soon as he got leave. I wondered whether the pretty young woman in the flat above us would see him. She always nodded so kindly to me and treated me as if I were quite grown-up. Once she had called out: "Oh please go on singing—you sing so beautifully!" What would she say when such a smart young soldier—a Cockchafer from the Guards too—came to see me!

When I knew that that charming Mrs. Kühnen was at home I used to sit down at the piano and start singing—a melody of folk songs and sentimental ballads—for I knew almost no classical music. And one day she came downstairs, sat down beside Mother and me and said: "Miss Lotte, the more I hear your beautiful voice the more I think it is wrong that you shouldn't have it trained. Wouldn't you like to be a singer?"

"Of course I should! But it's too expensive. Papa has already enrolled me at the commercial school and then perhaps I'll get into the Ritterschaft and eventually be eligible for a pension. Papa just can't let me study."

Frau Kühnen looked at me thoughtfully and Mamma said timidly: "It was always our wish that Lotte's voice should at least be tried out, but we don't really know where and how to do it."

"Oh I know how that could be done," cried Frau Kühnen briskly. "My uncle is lessee of the canteen at the Royal High School of Music where the students spend their free time—I'll ask him whether he can give us any advice."

The very next day she came back radiant with joy. "This looks like a piece of luck for you, Miss Lottchen: in a week the entrance examinations take place at the Hochschule. My uncle has spoken to Miss Erna Tiedke; she is a very advanced singing student who is already taking engagements. We are to go to her today, and she will hear you and decide whether we can risk entering you for the examination."

What an event! What should I sing? I didn't know any good music at all although I had twice been at the Opera, standing in the top gallery with Fritz and Willy. I had heard *Lohengrin* with Hiedler as Elsa and Grüning as Lohengrin—and the second time *Mignon* with Destinn. Nearly distracted I had listened to her angelic voice, thinking: "Oh dear—and they always said I ought to have my voice trained. I don't dare even to sing a folk song now that I've heard that voice down there . . ." and at home I locked up all the songs I had—for a time. . . .

But now, what was I to sing? Frau Kühnen consolingly said that Fräulein Tiedke would probably settle all that herself. So off we went with Mother's blessing, secretly behind

36

Father's back—he wouldn't have allowed such "nonsense," which might finally even spoil his plans for me, good solid plans. . . .

Erna Tiedke was a very superior-looking girl with wonderful red-gold curly hair, the delicate white skin of red-haired people and white lashes and brows. She loved behaving like a prima donna, wore a whole shopwindowful of imitation jewelry on her person and a shawl with long fringes decorated with ostrich feathers round her really magnificent shoulders. I thought she was simply fascinating and was so intimidated that I scarcely dared to breathe. Nor was I disturbed by the strong smell of warmed-up cabbage which didn't quite go with the sophistication of Erna's pungent scent. . . . To me she appeared as a higher being, red-gold and white, glowing and sparkling between the homely red plush curtains. . . .

Only half-conscious I sang after her what she sang to me in a voice as clear as a bell. Higher and higher she went—and desperately I went screaming after her thinking with absolute conviction, now she's going to throw me downstairs immediately and forbid me ever to bother her again—and my lovely dream of being a singer that I have had all my young life will be shattered forever.

"Congratulations on your top C," said Erna Tiedke dramatically breaking in on my gloomy prognostications. . . .

Although I thought darkly that there was no cause for

37

congratulations in that painfully squeaked-out top C, there was so much good will and encouragement in her words that tears sprang to my eyes.

"Oh do you think that I—and what do you think that I—"

"Yes, I certainly do. We've got one week before the examination—I'll soon take something through with you that you can sing there. It'll be all right. You have a very pretty voice."

Overwhelmed I stammered out some expression of eternal gratitude.

"My lessons cost two marks," said Erna Tiedke coolly, rearranging her many necklaces.

Poor Mother! I thought. Father must know nothing about this extravagant outlay. . . .

"For this audition I shall make an exception and charge you nothing," said Erna with the preoccupied air of a very busy singing teacher. "And now come back tomorrow and bring Siebel's aria from *Faust* and also the aria 'Jerusalem' from *Paulus*."

It was only when we were in the street that I became aware that in my utter confusion I had not said good-by. I was very worried about this. Indeed it seemed to me that my whole career was in jeopardy if my bad manners had perhaps aroused the wrath of the great Erna. . . .

But, thank goodness, she was quite friendly the next day—

38

and I started learning feverishly. We concentrated principally on the Jerusalem Lament, and she took great trouble
with me. It was by no means easy. There was hardly any
time for vocal exercises. So to make my rather light voice
sound fuller and thicker, I had to sing: "Jurusalem, thaat
killast tha prophats," which sounded very disenchanting to
me. But she was quite right to make me do this. What could
she do in such a short time? What trouble she had even to
make me sing properly in time! Rhythm was my weak point
and Willy often nearly lost his temper when I used to accompany his very nice violin-playing—on those lovely evenings in the Hochmeister Strasse—and always went wrong,
however lovingly he tried to follow me on his violin. The
latest Berlin song, "You are too pretty to be true," never
would come right. . . .

And now suddenly I found myself confronted with serious,
good music and had to stop singing "as I felt," and again
and again hear the impatient voice of my young singing
teacher saying: "Wrong, be more careful. You've no idea
of rhythm. Oh dear, how many things must I teach you in
six days. . . ."

Desperately I would swallow my tears, convinced that nothing would ever come of me and that Father was quite right
at home over this ridiculous nonsense that Frau Kühnen had
started when it was quite uncalled for. But he would come
along with me to the examination in the Hochschule, and if

39

the professors couldn't give him the assurance that I would become a good, capable singing teacher, then I would have to go to the commercial school without another word.

Suddenly the thought of the commercial school and the Ritterschaft rose before me like terrible black prison gates. . . . Hitherto I had never found it unpleasant to have to do as Father told me, but now a door to wonderland had opened to me in which shone the glorified form of Erna Tiedke, singing her brilliant trills and bewildering coloraturas and relating her dizzying conquests on her path to fame. . . . It seemed to me that every other coloratura-singer in the world was done for, and when I shyly asked Fräulein Tiedke who sang her parts in the Royal Opera house, she would answer with proud modesty: "As yet, Frau Herzog. . . ."

Incidentally I don't know what did become of her. She took an engagement soon after in a town in central Germany and I never heard any more of her, and later, when I tried to establish contacts I was unsuccessful. So many proud dreams are shattered! Many are called and few are chosen!

The day of the examination came. Father took me there. I was not particularly excited. I was accustomed to examinations from my not-too-distant school days. I "knew" my aria all right; the other, the Siebel aria, we had only run through once, just in case. I certainly wouldn't have to sing it, Erna Tiedke thought.

My heart sank considerably when I saw the large number that had come in the hope of being accepted. Well did I

40

know that only eight students came in question as there was no room for more that term, and about thirty-two were awaiting the examination.

"Don't worry," I whispered to Father, "that commercial school is a certainty."

But he just muttered something unintelligible and eyed my rivals with an inimical glare: his ambition was roused!

We were called up in alphabetical order, and a trick of fate ordained it that a great many came before me. And worst of all—the two girls just before me both sang "Jerusalem!" I listened attentively and thought they sang much better than I did. Then the high white door opened for me, and I stood before a long table at which a number of ladies and gentlemen were sitting looking at me. I nearly made a proper child's curtsey from sheer nervousness.

"Ah, this little lady has been learning with Erna Tiedke," cried one lanky old Father Christmas, stroking his bushy beard benevolently. It was Professor Adolf Schulze, the head of the singing department. He looked through the papers that I had had to send in, certificates of birth and baptism, school leaving-certificate and school report, and rang a bell at the same time. "Please ask Fraülein Tiedke to come here," he requested the fat dignified servitor with the silver buttons who looked to me as if he had stepped straight out of the Countess-novels of our childhood. Erna appeared. And then I saw that self-possessed person, now a student herself before a severe teaching staff, give a very shy greeting,

41

and I watched the transformation with curiosity. Professor Schulze drew her kindly down on a chair beside his—and there she sat, radiant as a child at this distinction, and nodded encouragingly to me. I believe she was far more excited than I was, for she was almost a professional already, conscious of her work and her responsibility—and so she trembled with ardent desire for success. While I was just a silly little goose that had learned its lesson and now wanted to show what it could do.

"What would you like to sing, young lady?" inquired the mild grandfatherly voice of the President.

" 'Jerusalem' from *Paulus.*"

A general protest rose from the staff table. They laughingly declined to hear the heart-rending lament a third time.

Erna Tiedke grew pale.

"But that's the only thing we've studied properly, Professor," she said in pleading tones; "we just went once through Siebel's aria."

"Bravo, let's have Siebel's aria!" came the interruption. "Go on!"

I looked into her light eyes, wide with fear, but found no encouragement there. "Oh it will be all right, I suppose?" I thought and began singing—and saw their gazes fixed on me, smiling and benevolent, and saw them nodding their heads and clapping Fräulein Tiedke approvingly on the back, and then I found myself outside with the summons to come for their decision the next day.

42

Erna rushed after me and folded me in her arms. . . .

"They've passed you, you little donkey," she said like a tomboy in her glee. . . .

Then she overwhelmed Father with stupendous prophecies for the future—whole groves of laurels would have to be felled for me, a castle on the sea would be the least of my humble dwellings and princes and millionaires would shoot each other for my sake.

Father listened in a daze and regarded with obvious suspicion this mercurial little person, who today in honor of my examination had appeared in all her war paint and fairly glittered with brilliants.

"I hope Lotte can be trained as a good, capable singing teacher," he said cautiously.

"No, she must go on the stage."

"I shall be a concert-singer," I resolved ecstatically.

But first I must tell Mother and Fritz all about it!

And Willy, who had just lately listened with a certain skepticism to my enthusiastic description of my singing lesson when he came on his first visit to us in Lichterfelde, now he'd get a surprise! I was a student like him!

"Papa, may I have visiting cards printed with 'student of music'?" I asked in the tram going home.

"That would be an entirely superfluous item of expenditure," Father answered with a shake of the head. "In any case I must first find out tomorrow from official sources what your prospects are—whether you can reckon on a free grant, because if it's a question of a hundred and fifty marks, where could I get hold of them?"

That silenced me. In my joy I hadn't thought of that: teaching does cost money, and I knew only too well that it must cost us nothing. It was bad enough that presumably I wouldn't be earning anything for a few years. But then— later! Erna Tiedke simply juggled with the millions that could be earned by singing! But Father refused to listen.

"That's all just talk," he countered. "You won't charm any bird from the tree that way. Of course you sang well. I was listening: no one sang as well as you."

Dear good Father! He kept this opinion to the end of his life. Later, whoever it was that was singing, no matter what star came, saw and conquered, the conclusion of every pæan of praise was always, "but no one can sing like Lotte." How impatient and cross this subjectivity would make me, and how often, out of sheer contrariness, I would praise the other singer to the sky just to make him stop. And now, when his voice is forever stilled, how gladly would I hear those dear, proud, fatherly words. . . .

The next day there were still fearful moments of anxious expectation: at last Father and I stood before Professor Schulze in his office. Trembling with joy I heard the official corroboration of my admission into the Royal Hochschule. He advised me to attend as many lectures as possible—how my heart beat with pride at that academic word—particularly those on Italian, theory and elocution. My singing teacher would be Fräulein Helene Jordan; he knew I would be in good hands. Then came the burning question: would I get a scholarship? Professor Schulze replied with a decided negative. According to the rules, a scholarship was only possible after one term at the school. The gift of God alone could not be rewarded, industry and assiduity must also count. I choked for breath. I did not dare look at Father. Now he'll say no, I thought in distress. But no, Father tentatively inquired as to my future prospects.

"Well, I think your little daughter will be a fine oratorio-singer one day."

Aha, this was something new—I pricked up my ears, for soon any kind of singing would be ruled out. . . .

"Oratorio is the finest and noblest branch of singing," said the grandfatherly voice with emotion, "for Heaven's sake don't let your dear good child go on the stage. She certainly wouldn't be suited for it. As an oratorio and concert-singer she could teach as well and have a solid income. . . ."

"Is there any possibility of a State job for her—with a pension?" asked Father with timid hope.

"Why not, my dear Mr. Lehmann? Take my advice, have her voice trained. She'll always be able to earn her daily bread with her voice, her talent and—I trust—also by her diligence."

Father nodded agreement—and the two good, solicitous family-fathers shook hands with understanding.

45

"Oh Heavens, Papa, what'll we do about the hundred and fifty marks?" I said anxiously once we were outside— for my father's acquiescence seemed almost criminally reckless to me. He gave a deep sigh: "I don't know yet. I'll manage to scrape it up. That Professor Schulze is a very reasonable man, I liked him very much and I'm sure his advice is good. So we'll just have to find the money."

Unfortunately this indulgent mood of Father's didn't last long. They gave him to understand at the Ritterschaft that one didn't let one's daughter study if one wasn't in a position to do so, and that he couldn't count on a loan or even an advance from them. So Father lost all courage and interest and wanted to have nothing more to do with "the whole business." Those were bad days at home, and I could scarcely have won through by myself if my mother hadn't stood courageously by me, determined to fulfill her daughter's every wish. And Fritz too was my most ardent supporter. He who had learned to renounce so much and who knew what it meant to have to give something up, wove all his dreams round my life and lived only for the idea that "I should become something great." He suffered privations for me all the years of my studies, he lived every phase of my progress with me, he rejoiced in my joys and sorrowed over my disappointments. With the entire impetuous vehemence of his character which knew no moderation he took up the idea of my career. Without him, without his help I should have only too often given it up and ruefully relapsed into a

46

practical profession. . . . The money was procured, I no longer remember how. Did Fritz raise it? In any case there it was, the term was paid for and I was now a "student of music."

Immediately I felt a strange transformation, which really made me feel ashamed, in my feelings toward my good Willy. He had written very happily to say how glad he was about my utterly unexpected success in the examination, and that he knew very well that the duties of my profession would not make me neglect my duties to house and home. This honest, well-meaning letter roused my deepest displeasure.

"What does he mean, duties to house and home?" I thought, deeply offended. "Does he mean me to beat carpets in the morning and give concerts at night?"

And all the high-sounding phrases I had heard from Erna Tiedke came up in my mind: "I must dedicate my life to Art! Nothing must divert me from my lofty goal! I must belong to the world as a priestess of Art—" thus I apostrophized myself.

In a mood of lofty renunciation I wrote Willy a farewell letter and my stupid faithless heart scarcely quickened a beat—I only thought I was tremendously interesting. . . . It was only right at the end of the letter that I hesitated and then added, very stupidly and childishly: "But if you will agree to my loving you less than my Art, I will go on being engaged to you."

Willy, however, sent me a very cool letter saying he would

47

make no compromises and that our ways had better part. . . .
I certainly shed a few hot tears over his farewell letter—but
a new life was beginning for me, in which each day was
packed with exciting new sensations, so I soon forgot and
plunged headlong into my Art.

My Art! Bold words! It consisted meantime of a pretty,
natural little voice. . . .

CHAPTER
FIVE

FRÄULEIN HELENE JORDAN, my new singing teacher, was a dear sympathetic woman who took a great interest in me and began to train my voice with great patience. It really was very boring, this business of breathing and progressing by slow degrees. Everything was too slow for my impatient mind. I used to stand longingly at the doors of the opera class taken by Professer Felix Schmidt, and listen to the voices of Erna Tiedke and the other "great ones," who would soon be allowed to take engagements, and for whom the laurel bushes were already growing in the south. . . .

It was painful to be so new, so ridiculously young, such a beginner. Once, when a bass from the opera class, a friend of Erna Tiedke's, was going past me, he cried: "Well little lamb, can you say baa yet?" I burst into tears of bitterest mortification.

Fräulein Jordan laughed. "Good Heavens," she said, "she's crying because she's too young! Isn't Mr. Niels right? Aren't you really a silly little baa-lamb? Being too young is a mistake, only too quickly corrected, unfortunately!"

49

And she was still smiling to herself long after I had diligently started my sol-fa again.

The elocution classes were wonderful. The clear enunciation of my singing has frequently been praised and I believe that I owe this chiefly to Fräulein Elise Bartels, who took the elocution class. We learned to formulate every vowel consciously and fundamentally, and every consonant was shaped and polished. The first poem that we read in its entirety was Chamisso's "Salas y Gomez." I still enjoy reciting this verse slowly to myself as we used to have to do, tasting every syllable delicately on our tongues like a rare fruit:

> *"Salas y Gomez raget aus den Fluten*
> *Des stillen Meers, ein Felsen, kahl und bloss,*
> *Besonnt von scheitelrechter Sonne Gluten,*
> *Ein Steingestell ohn' alles Gras und Moos,*
> *Das sich das Volk der Vogel auserkor*
> *Zur Ruhstatt im bewegten Meeresschoss...."*

(Salas y Gomez towers above the floods of quiet seas, a bare and barren cliff exposed to the direct rays of the sun, a stony mass devoid of grass or moss, serving as a refuge for the feathered race upon the heaving bosom of the sea....)

Fräulein Bartels, a most energetic person with short-cropped hair, suffered no slipshod ways. And woe to the unfortunate with no natural "rolled *r*" which is essential for

50

elocution and singing! The poor soul would shed many tears over the terrible tongue-twisting exercises that had to be done until the most masterly *r* had been achieved and the dreaded sentence, *"Roland der Ries' am Rathaus zu Bremen"* (Roland the Giant at the town hall of Bremen), satisfactorily pronounced.

While I made good progress in Italian too, and worked diligently at piano, I was a thorn in the side of my theory professor, Herr van Eyken—just as at school I was hopeless at arithmetic! Finally I would constantly urge him to give me up as a bad job, as he could see I was just too stupid to understand a thing about it. His embittered assent did not offend me in the least. . . .

At the end of the first term a test performance took place in the large hall. I sang the lovely Schumann song, "What will the lonely tear." Then I had the privilege of going to Professor Schulze and receiving the joyful information that I had won a free scholarship at the Hochschule to the end of my studies.

It was high time that some ray of sunshine came to brighten our home. Mother was seriously ill. Fritz served his year with the Rifle Brigade at Lichterfelde, a very grand regiment but the most practical one for him as he could live at home and save considerably in this way. He couldn't afford a servant so Mother used to brush up his heavy uniform with the help of the daily-woman. And what a lot there was to be washed and ironed! I always had to look clean and tidy too, and one of my two wash-blouses was always hanging up to dry in the loft. And while Father was sitting in his office, Fritz doing his training and I learning at the Hochschule, Mother overtaxed her strength so severely that finally a bad gastric hemorrhage kept her in bed for weeks. So of course there was no more thought of studying for me! I was given leave at the Hochschule with the assurance that my scholarship would remain open, and my anxious concern for Mamma and the household, which I knew very little about, made me forget all dreams of the future. I had to do the cooking—and we were too sad even to laugh at the bewildering specimens of my culinary art. . . . But I always felt very bitter at the despairing faces that were made when yet another dish, constructed entirely according to the cook book, was served up. But one learns everything in time, and so luckily I eventually managed to make a *schnitzel* that really looked like a *schnitzel* and an omelet that no longer flapped about like a dying fish at the first touch of the spoon. . . . When Mother, who was always worrying, inquired whether everyone was getting enough to eat, we nodded assent, and then they would all praise my unsuspected culinary talents so that a happy smile of contentment flitted across her pale face. How proud she was of her clever daughter!

When she had slowly recovered and things got back to normal again, I was able to go back to the Hochschule. I had missed a great deal and had to work very hard to make up

My Parents in Westerland.

for it. I plunged into my work with redoubled zeal. When my brother had finished his year's service it was a great relief to us all. Moreover Father was lucky enough to secure a post as superintendent quite near, so we had a fine rent-free flat in the Augusta Strasse with a wonderful loggia and a little front garden where we felt very happy. A sweet little spaniel called Lulu became our beloved house companion. Unfortunately it had a habit of defending us so fierily against everyone that we often had complaints that he snapped at people, and we made him listen to long lectures which he did with rapturous tail-waggings. . . .

In the tram I often met a girl of my own age who also went to the Hochschule. One day we started talking. She was born in Australia, was called Eyleen, and was studying violin. She was very nice, and I found her foreign accent simply fascinating. The next day she was sitting in the tram again, but she looked right through me. I couldn't understand it and looked inquiringly at her, when she suddenly said with a blush: "Excuse me, are you a singing student called Lotte Lehmann? Did you speak to Eyleen yesterday? I'm her twin sister Jessie. We are so like each other that everyone gets us mixed."

I stared at her, speechless. I couldn't have believed such a resemblance possible. Jessie and Eyleen—I soon struck up an intimate friendship with both of them, full of conflicts in so far as I never really knew which of them I liked better. . . .

Perhaps this likeness was due a little to the fact that they were beings from a different, fascinating and imposing world—brought up in comfortable, even wealthy circumstances. . . . How impressed I was when one of them said: "No, you can't meet us every day on the tram, we only use it when Mother has the car."

"What car?" I asked with a sudden presentiment.

"Our own car," was the indifferent answer.

A car!

I was speechless.

The epitome of all riches, the dream of all my most secret dreams, for how could one ever express such audacity in words?

And now? Here was a car—taken quite as a matter of course. . . . What a day that was when I was taken for the first time in the lovely glittering vehicle, and Quandt, the chauffeur, held the door open for me when I shyly wished him "Good-morning." What a day! And the day I was invited to my first meal with my new friends, and their mother, a slim, elegant woman with close-cropped curls, a typical Englishwoman in her whole mode of life, came briskly up to me and greeted me with an English, "How do you do?" I was so confused I couldn't recall a single word of my school English and only answered with a scarcely audible German, "Quite well thank you."

At table we were waited on by two neat maids in black dresses with little white caps and gloves—and everything

54

tasted really twice as good when it was served on silver dishes....

I wonder whether it was all as extravagant and luxurious as I thought? Today I can't really tell and I scarcely think so. But I certainly thought so at the time: after all it was the first time I had ever come across a family where money was never mentioned and where it was all the same whether fees were one thousand or ten thousand marks.

Eyleen was always very frail and delicate. When she was going through one of her many operations she got into a strange state of mental disorder. As she couldn't bear any-one near her but Jessie and myself I came to stay with them at the worst period of her illness and helped to nurse her. Bad and disquieting were those hours at poor pale thin Eyleen's bedside, when her eyes shone with an unearthly light and she stared and talked at forms that existed only in her poor disordered mind.

This nursing with all its terrors had a bad effect on my nerves and finally the doctor diagnosed a nervous heart, and in decisive manner urgently recommended me to go and take a cure at Bad Liebenstein, otherwise there were grave doubts as to whether I could continue with my studies. Kind Professor Schulze saw to it that I got a tidy sum of money from the Hochschule for "recuperation-pay" and this, with our modest requirements—Mother came with me—sufficed for a cure which fully restored me to health.

Through some childish quarrel I became estranged from

the two sisters. I no longer remember what foolishness caused the breakup of our friendship. When I met Jessie by chance in London quite recently we racked our brains in vain over the real cause of our separation, but she couldn't remember either. Since her marriage Jessie has lived in London with her pretty, adored boy, and has made a name for herself as a pianist. And Eyleen, dear, delicate Eyleen died long ago; she was terribly burned in an accident, and I have only a little picture of her from those early times—with her fiddle under her arm. . . .

In the middle of summer we always managed to go away to the Baltic. Quite by chance we had heard of a little island where we could live more cheaply than in Berlin, so that our third-class fares scarcely counted. This beloved, incredibly beautiful and enchanting isle is called Hiddensee—and from my first visit there I have been a victim for all times to this little plot of earth. I always return to it and today, even though it is a fairly popular summer resort, I still know places of heavenly remoteness and beauty.

At that time the island was mostly visited by artists—all down the rocky coast, known as the Hiddensee Riviera, one came across solitary painters in long white smocks working away furiously—hopelessly attempting to catch the indescribable magic of those gently sloping hills sinking into the white sands of the shore, the steep gullies where the wild terns circled and screamed, the stark gold-laden clumps of broom at the edge of the wood. . . .

56

Weeks of enchanting beauty we used to spend there, and when the good old steamer *Caprivi* brought us back to Stralsund again, I was always sunburned and rested, full of new vigor and joy.

In my second year my singing teacher, Fräulein Jordan, took influenza with such serious consequences that she was given indefinite leave. So I went to another teacher and the change did me no good. I got badly stuck in my studies and, in addition, I began to feel quite purposeless, for Professor Schulze kept advising me to specialize in oratorio for which I had not the slightest inclination. The desire to go on the stage had long since awakened in me. Actually I had arrived at it in quite a different way from so many people: most of them started off with the loftiest dreams which grew more humble as their studies progressed. Girls who once had the definite wish to take the world by storm as celebrated prima donnas, were later quite glad to have a good testimonial that would bring them singing pupils and small concert engagements. I had started off with very humble aims, and it was only very gradually that ambitious desires awoke in me and became more and more clear until at last they would not leave hold of me and I knew that there was only one vocation for me—the stage! But the development of my voice, whose timbre was constantly praised, did not keep pace with my dreams. I felt that I wasn't on the right road and often discussed it for hours with my brother Fritz. I had once been greatly impressed by a performance given by

57

Etelka Gerster's singing class. Frau Gerster was the head of a private school and a very well-known singing teacher, a pupil of Marchesi. One day I plucked up courage and wrote to her, wrote and told her all my troubles—saying that I had no money to pay for an expensive course with her, but earnestly begging her to let me have an audition and perhaps give me a scholarship. Father regarded my efforts with displeasure, declared all studying a waste of time, and said he considered a secretary's post would be the most sensible and worth-while aim in life for me. But I was completely obsessed by my idea.

"Leave me alone, Papa," I said in tears. "I don't want to live if everything has been in vain. Let me just try, and do believe that we'll find a way. Don't let us give it all up!"

Fritz stood by me like a lioness over its young. And so the letter was dispatched.

Fearful days of waiting followed! At last came an answer: Fräulein Eva Reinhold, one of the mistresses in the Gerster School of Singing, wrote that I was to come and sing to her at the Mæstra's request. Well did I know how much depended on this! Everything, my entire future and happiness rested on that decisive half-hour when I sang to friendly, dark-haired Fräulein Reinhold. After the first song she said: "Fräulein Lehmann, Frau Gerster doesn't give scholarships at her school on principle. But she will give you an audition. In any case don't worry: I will take you on privately as a non-paying pupil as I scarcely think Frau Gerster will. You have

58

a beautiful voice that is well worth training. Come tomorrow to Frau Gerster. I shall be there too."

I could scarcely speak for gratitude and joy, and I tremblingly kissed the hand she graciously extended. Little did I dream that the very woman who that day so benevolently delivered me from a great fear would one day plunge me into the darkest hours of my young life.

The next morning I stood in Etelka Gerster's elegant flat before the Mæstra. I sang—and saw her say something with a smile to Fräulein Reinhold, and the look she gave me through her gold lorgnettes was very benevolent.

"You have a beautiful voice, Fräulein Lehmann," she said kindly, "and I will make a great exception and give you free tuition at my school. You will study with Fräulein Reinhold, and later I will take you myself." With a nod and a smiling look, Frau Gerster cut short my thanks.

At home, everyone shared in my happiness. Even Father saw that my future as a singer didn't appear to be quite hopeless and was glad of this solution and glad to see me laugh again. Mother clasped me weeping in her arms, and Fritz—he was the happiest of us all!

CHAPTER
SIX

THEN began another period of serious, concentrated study. The whole style of this school of singing was entirely different from that of the Royal Academy. Here there were swarms of foreigners wanting to learn singing in exchange for vast numbers of dollars, elegant extravagant creatures whom I gazed at open-mouthed. There was one simply lovely girl I always used to watch with shy delight: Betty Kalisch, who afterward married Felix Weingartner. She was one of Frau Gerster's favorites. Nobody paid any attention to me, of course. I stood at the doors, feeling very much of a stranger, quite overwhelmed with all the elegance, beauty and self-possession round about me.

Fräulein Reinhold took the business of singing very seriously. We had to sing with a little stick jammed between our teeth to accustom us always to keep our mouths equally wide open (a method of which I do not approve because, among other things, it makes the tone rigid and robs it of the loveliest quality one can strive for—the quality of flexibility.)

60

At first it was most difficult to keep the stick in place; every few minutes it would slip out of one's teeth, a constant source of suppressed joy to the other pupils attending the lesson. Fräulein Reinhold had not much sense of humor for that sort of thing. One day she asked a charming young American who took particular pleasure in roaring with laughter at the refractory stick: "Do you actually sing to learn something, or for your pleasure and mine?"

"Oh," answered the pretty little miss, "it's Mother who wants me to learn singing. I shall never sing for my own pleasure, I shall sing for Mother's pleasure." Which certainly was disarming. . . .

There was great excitement one day when the aged Mæstra, Marchesi, came to Berlin. A tea was given in her honor, and for the first time in my life I, together with all the other pupils, received an invitation to a grand reception. I squeezed myself shyly into a corner where with beating heart I watched all those delighted-looking ladies shaking hands as cordially as if it had been an unexpected pleasure to see one another there. A feeling of sadness overcame me. Would I ever learn to conduct myself in this easy, self-possessed manner, to feel that I belonged and not so out of it and sure to be in everyone's way if I didn't squeeze myself into the most out-of-the-way corner? . . .

Then they started singing. Julia Culp's wonderful voice floated in silver streams through the room and everyone else who sang rivaled her in beauty of tone and expression. At

61

least so it seemed to me and I thought: "Oh, I'll never learn to sing like that!" . . . And the afternoon that gave pleasure to so many made me deeply dejected.

During this time I returned to Perleberg only once. The president of the Perleberg Women's Institute was Frau von Saldern, the wife of the Ritterschaft director who had been Papa's chief in our Perleberg days. So now I appeared on the concert platform before an audience of my townsfolk. I stayed with Frau von Saldern; that is, in the principal Ritterschaft building next door to our dear old house which looked like a lost paradise to me. Everything had changed so much: the Saldern's house I had once regarded as a wealthy mansion filled with costly and unaccessible objects—and now I passed through its rooms with a slightly disillusioned feeling: so this was what the world was really like? A suite of quite pretty rooms awaited me, stripped of all enchantment—for now I had seen grander and lovelier rooms. I was almost sorry to have my memories spoiled. But our garden and our dear old house, they still looked like home. Yet not for a single moment did I long to be back in the little town where I had grown up.

Shortly after, Frau von Saldern wrote and told me I was to have an audition in the near future with Baron zu Putlitz, the general director of the Stuttgart Court Theater. I was very grateful and excited—for now the possibility of an engagement was actually approaching and this to me meant not only the gate to the achievement of all my hopes, but

62

also a possibility of at last earning money and easing the burden that my parents and my brother had borne for my sake.

Fräulein Reinhold was not very pleased with this idea, as she rightly considered that I was not really ready to take engagements yet, but she finally recommended me to Professor Bake who was kind enough to coach me in Agathe's aria from the *Freischütz* and "Elsa's Dream" from *Lohengrin* without taking any payment. Herr Bake, an excellent concert-accompanist, did his utmost to instill into me the rhythm that I lacked. I was in constant conflict with all note values and in the excitement of singing I kept forgetting, in spite of arduous practicing, to think of the beat I didn't really feel. So Herr Bake was not particularly enchanted by me either, and earnestly discussed this grievous lack of mine with Fräulein Reinhold.

"She probably doesn't practice enough," she said with a severe look.

Herr Bake shrugged his shoulders: "Possibly she doesn't work hard enough. What a pity—her voice is so beautiful and promising."

I stood there, pale and covered with shame. So it came to this: I must practice harder—although I always had worked really hard.

The audition surpassed all expectations. In the salon of a large Berlin hotel Baron Putlitz heard me and gave my voice quite exceptional praise. He showed a great interest in me

63

and said I might write to him when I considered accepting engagements so that we might have another audition and then come to a definite agreement. I went home very happy, filled with gratitude toward Herr Bake who had accompanied me and steered me cautiously past all the dangerous reefs of rhythmic uncertainty. . . .

In spite of this success I did not feel happy with this singing method. It is generally an enormous stroke of luck to find a teacher who will give a voice individual training. What is right for one is not right for all! I had heard pupils who had made the most marvelous progress there and for whom that method of singing seemed to be made. For me it certainly wasn't the right one. I felt myself fettered and chained the whole time, singing became difficult—and I felt that the training I was having was so contrary to my natural instincts that I simply had to force myself to sing as I was supposed to. We had exercise sheets with the three vocal registers, chest voice, middle register and head voice, printed in different colors. The voice fairly leaped audibly from one register to another, a thing I couldn't agree with, for to me a steady flow of tone was the highest possible aim. Amid doubts and despair I struggled on—for if things were to go wrong here, where would I find a way?

In summer, on Fräulein Reinhold's recommendation, I went to stay with friends of hers. I spent enchanting weeks with Frau von Poser in Schweidnitz, where she lived with her husband, an officer of high rank in the regiment stationed there, and her charming, well-mannered little boy, in a lovely house with a huge garden—a real "park!" I was welcomed with warm-hearted affection, not for a moment regarded as a protégée but rather as a really welcome companion—such was the atmosphere that surrounded me. I still feel deeply indebted to that dear, fine woman, and am always glad when, in summer during the Salzburg Festival, I can visit her and her husband, now a retired general, at their lovely place, Castle Grubhof.

Full of gratitude, I went back to work and tried by continuous application to understand what seemed incomprehensible to me. My zeal and industry did not flag—but my joyous courage did, that firm confidence which is the best foundation for solid work. Fräulein Reinhold began to grow impatient. For weeks and weeks we worked at the same thing, "Dove sono," the Countess's big aria in *Figaro*. Psychologically it would have been more correct if Fräulein Reinhold had laid aside for a while this aria which simply refused to come right, and had taken up something else with me and come back to it later. But she did things differently. She wanted to make it come. Day after day, week after week, the alpha and the omega of the singing lesson was this aria before which my inability rose to an *idée fixe* and became such a nervous phobia that even at the first chords of the recitative my knees would start trembling. Shortly before the New Year—I had studied for about a year with her—Fräulein Reinhold informed me with a black look that Frau

65

Gerster wanted to hear me again. I can scarcely remember anything about that audition. I sang in a semi-conscious condition—I no longer remember what. Whether it was the *Freischütz* aria that had won me the friendly praise of the Stuttgart director or the Countess's aria that haunted my dreams in torturing dissonance—I don't know. All I remember is cold eyes, shoulders shrugged crushingly—and when I closed the doors of the elegant Gerster School behind me after a "good afternoon" that was received in silence, I knew that they would never open again to me. . . .

I wrote to Fräulein Reinhold—a letter filled with desperate questions, accusations and self-denunciations. I knew, of course, that she wouldn't go on teaching me now—but why had she made me keep on at that one aria and not tried something else? Did she want to have nothing more to do with me? Had she at least sufficient regard for me to recommend me to another teacher? I couldn't live without my work—without the hope of becoming an artist. And I begged her—I beseeched her to help me, not to leave me in the lurch. The next day—it was New Year's Eve—Fräulein Reinhold asked me to come round to her home. She stood before me—oh, so strange and unapproachable! Her eyes were fixed on me, harsh and severe, and harsh and severe were the words with which she condemned me. Frau Gerster had been most dissatisfied, I had sung very badly and done her no credit. My studies were now at an end, she knew of nothing for me, and—good-by.

66

I stood on the stairs for a time in a sort of daze and everything went round me. On my way home to Lichterfelde the wheels of the suburban train no longer sang the old childhood song: "I think I can—I knew I could" . . . oh no. They kept thumping out the same thing, Fräulein Reinhold's hard angry "good-by." Good-by to my lovely dreams! Good-by to all hope! Good-by to all happiness!

At home I couldn't find words to tell them everything. Dumb and silent I sat at table until a messenger came with a parcel for me and out of the wrappings fell the sofa cushion I had made for Fräulein Reinhold at Christmas and the following letter:

"Dear Fräulein Lehmann:

"I shall speak to your father today on behalf of Frau Gerster, but I should like to write you a few lines. I am sorry that your singing instruction at the Gerster School has come to an end in this way, but alas! I have seen this coming for months. I can only say that none of my pupils has ever been such a disappointment as you have, and this has given me many a dark hour. I believe that, if you want to and have to achieve something in the future, you should take up a practical career. Only then will you come to know the real meaning of hard work, and perhaps you will realize later that you weren't doing your duty with all your might. Whether you were considered a hard worker at the Hochschule you will know best yourself. Finally, I have one request

67

to make. It is very painful for me to keep this cushion you gave me, now that you are no longer my pupil. You have taken great trouble over it and I am sure you will be able to make use of it elsewhere. I don't want to hurt your feelings, Fräulein Lehmann, but I really cannot keep it. The feeling that you had made any sacrifice for me would be painful to me. Now I know that the only sacrifice that you and your parents made during your year's study at Frau Gerster's School of Singing was only a matter of ten or twelve marks, and that you were unfortunately unable to appreciate the value of your tuition—for which others pay sixty marks a month—its true worth. Frau Gerster requests me to tell you that your progress is not even that of a mediocre pupil, *and that even as a paying pupil you would have been expelled.* Free tuition in her school is only for girls of exceptional attainments, moreover Frau Gerster was extremely surprised at the tone of your letter to me. She says that I have done more with you by my great patience in teaching you than she could have expected, for otherwise you would have been dismissed from her School of Singing several months ago. How could you expect me ever to recommend you to any other member of the staff in the school when Herr Bake found your industry unsatisfactory.

"With all good wishes for your future, Fräulein Lehmann and kindest regards

"I am, Yours sincerely,

"Eva Reinhold."

So there I was with nothing left for me—all hope, all longing at an end. I was so completely paralyzed in my innermost being that I couldn't even cry. I was actually too healthy to faint, but my mind was in a sort of daze. I could neither think nor feel nor even wish for anything. Mother helped me to bed crying and sat beside me, desperately seeking some word of comfort. Father fell silent when he looked at me and all his "I told you so's" remained unsaid. And Fritz? He stayed with me until daybreak, long after my parents were asleep and I had found relief in tears that would no longer be denied. It certainly sounds sentimental when I tell it, but it is nevertheless true: the New Year's chimes outside sounded like a death knell to me. Everything for me was at an end. Even Fritz, who had never lost courage and never even allowed the thought that I might have to give up my studies to enter the realm of possibilities, even he had nothing to suggest. And so we kept on saying to each other that we must be sensible and realize where we stood, it was all over now and we must pull ourselves together. . . .

What was I going to do? I shuddered at the thought of bare office walls and shyly suggested: "Don't you think I could get a post as companion? I imagine it might be quite nice to be with some aristocratic old lady and read and sing to her—I'd be good enough for that," I added bitterly.

Fritz agreed enthusiastically, glad that I had expressed any opinion whatsoever about the future. He brought the

69

newspaper really with the idea of distracting me and we looked through the "vacant situations" column to see if we could find a suitable one.

"It would be best," said Fritz, "for us to put in an advertisement. We could word it just as you like."

And we sent in an advertisement that sounded very alluring to us. I was quite keen about it—but I often caught myself thinking: "Is it really for me we're trying to find a job? Is it possible? Won't some miracle come and save me? Is this really the end of everything?"

Yes, it was the end. I must learn to realize it. All this listening for the bell to ring in the next few days bringing a letter or a telegram was useless. Slowly the days crawled by, gradually my heart ceased its wild beating at every step on the stairs, ordinary every-day life returned and with it the increasingly urgent problem—what was I to do?

Father was against my becoming a companion and pleaded the cause of a secretaryship with the old fervor. I soon yielded—it was really all the same to me what I was going to be. So Father entered my name for the next course at the commercial school which was due to begin, I believe, on January 15. I listened in silence with downcast eyes while he urged me to believe that I would be very happy in that profession and one day would have forgotten all about this silly singing business.

"No," I cried suddenly—and all this yielding-to-the-inevitable was swept away as if by a storm—"no, I can't—I can't!

70

As Sieglinde in *Die Walküre*.

Believe me—I simply can't! I'll try once again—just once more! I'll write to Frau Mallinger." I had seldom seen Father so angry. This unreasonableness verged on sheer stupidity! Didn't I realize that Fräulein Reinhold was probably quite right? Did I imagine it was the teacher's fault if I didn't make any progress? Wasn't I rather forced to believe that I really hadn't any talent? But his patience was at an end—the commercial school for me—and that was final!

I didn't say a word, but sat at the table and wrote—to Mathilde Mallinger who, after a great career as a famous opera-singer in Berlin and at Bayreuth, had a singing school of high repute in Berlin. I wrote page after page, telling her everything—even my own doubts of my talent, my perplexities, Fräulein Reinhold's and Frau Gerster's devastating condemnation, the frightful business of being expelled. . . . I didn't ask for free tuition—I knew that it was absolutely hopeless as she had to earn her living—but I begged her to give me an audition and perhaps recommend me to some advanced pupil.

Father looked at me, amazed at this obstinacy so foreign to my nature. He roared indignantly at my wasting a penny stamp on this useless letter—but then he went out very thoughtfully, and through all his anger there glimmered an affectionate fatherly look, full of solicitude for me.

I quickly took the letter to the mailbox with the bitter thought: "This penny stamp is really the last I shall waste on my happiness."

71

Life again held something for me—a new hope. When, after a few days, I received a letter from Mathilde Mallinger summoning me to go and see her, all my doubts and troubles vanished. I lived only for the one hour that was to decide everything.

CHAPTER
SEVEN

I T WAS a real artist's home that I entered: the walls were
covered with photographs, ribbons and faded laurels.
In one frame was a silver laurel wreath and beside it on a
yellowed card: "To the immortal Elsa—Ludwig II." My
heart nearly stopped beating with emotion.

Frau Mallinger, a stately old lady, came up to me vivaci-
ously. "Come, little misery," she said, with a kind smile,
"don't tell me anything but do the only thing that counts
here—sing!"

There were a lot of pupils sitting round listening curiously,
but after a few moments Frau Mallinger sent them all away.
"Come back tomorrow, I must talk to this child here for a
few minutes," she called after them.

And then something remarkable happened: the Mallinger
sang to me—and the whole time I felt: "Yes, that's how it
ought to be! Yes that's the way!" and I found the right way
myself and felt my voice pour from my throat freer than
ever before.

The old lady's big, beautiful eyes laughed at me. "Oh my

child, how beautiful! What did you say—no talent? No talent? I'll show you!" Then her face fell: "Yes, but I can't teach you for nothing—I have many obligations. How shall we manage it?"

She stood thinking and I could hear my heart beat in the silence.

"But come again, dear child. You can attend my classes— and one can learn a great deal from listening. And now and then I'll find time to do something about you. Well then— good-by until tomorrow. Come when you like—I am teaching all day."

I scarcely know how I got home. To be able to study again! And even if it only meant listening to classes I had read enough in those shining eyes to know that she would really help me!

Father regarded me today with special excitement. And when I had poured out everything and Mother and Fritz had said that this business of going to classes was certain to be just a beginning and who could tell whether it mightn't develop into getting really proper teaching, then Father said, and all the little wrinkles round his eyes danced in a happy smile: "I am all for you becoming a regular pupil of hers."

We were thunderstruck!

"Yes but Papa, you heard what I said—she doesn't give free tuition."

"That doesn't matter—then you'll just have to pay."

74

We looked at each other speechless. And then Father told his story.

Oh, he hadn't been idle! He had noticed how unreasonably I clung to the idea of going on the stage, so he had written to the Baron Konrad zu Putlitz, the brother of the Stuttgart manager, the owner of the ancient heritage of Gross-Pankow in Priegnitz. Father, who knew him officially from Perleberg days, had written and told him about me, including the fact that I had sung to his brother and had earned the gracious praise of His Excellency. Would it be possible to obtain a sum of money through the agency of the manager that would enable me to continue my studies to their conclusion? Baron Putlitz, a great patron of the arts, had made inquiries of his brother as to my talent, and the information he had received was so satisfactory that he had asked my father to go and see him—he was often in Berlin in his capacity of president of some agricultural society—and had told him that he would pay for my studies himself until I got professional engagements.

That was the miracle—it had actually happened!

Had I become a great author as my schoolteacher used to predict when I was a child, I should now be able to describe the happiness I now felt! But I can't. Life was restored again to me. That is all I can say!

The letter containing my painful efforts to express my thanks brought an invitation from Baroness Putlitz, who desired to make the acquaintance of the newest protégée. I found a lovable woman, used to concealing her warmhearted-ness behind a mask of dry severity, two tall pretty daughters with the shimmering corn-colored hair of all the Putlitzes, and the Baron himself, one of the greatest idealists I have ever met, a man of great imagination and depth of mind, tall, slim, fair, ineffably aristocratic, with blue eyes that re-vealed the whole of his great, benevolent soul. Tongue-tied with happiness and with my inability to thank them as I wanted to, for I simply couldn't find words, I sat at the tea table. The Baroness exhorted me, in a kind and motherly way, to do absolutely everything that was necessary for my studies. They were all looking forward already to hearing me, and I must come soon and sing to them. How gladly I made that promise! How gladly I went again—and how happy I was when my benefactors thought that my voice was beautiful and highly promising.

I made terrific progress with the Mallinger. My voice fairly blossomed! Every lesson gave it fresh qualities, and although the Mæstra in her exalted way which knew no half-measure would sometimes throw the book away with a curse and cry: "Go and learn how to darn stockings, silly goose, you are entirely devoid of talent"—I knew she didn't really mean it. And the tears which I was always ready to shed were not bitter ones, for they were dried by just as exagger-ated words of praise.

How wonderful it was when she could be induced to tell us stories from her rich store of reminiscences. What bril-

76

liant days she had seen! She sang Eva in the first performance of *Meistersinger,* and would relate with pride her nicest experience with Richard Wagner.

"We had a tremendous number of rehearsals for the Field of Song, and over and over again had to repeat the incident where I finally place the wreath on Walter Stolzing's brow. In my impatience I put in a trill—just for fun—where I have to sing the phrase 'Not one so clear a right hath shown,' and Wagner looked at me and laughed and said: 'Let her have her fun. We'll keep the trill since Mallinger likes it so much.' And so I really helped to compose the *Meistersinger.*"

How I drank in every word! I could have listened for hours. But then the old lady would give me a rap on the nose and say: "Come along, back to work! Gossiping won't teach you anything, my child!" And so we would go on singing and learning.

I studied with Mathilde Mallinger for about a year—and this year really first revealed the potentialities of my voice. She was the right teacher for me. I soon began studying my first rôle, that of Agathe in the *Freischütz.* I was coached in it by Herr Arndt, who at that time was still Mallinger's coach and is now a long-established and successful singing master in Berlin. His were no ordinary coaching lessons, for he actually continued one's singing instruction and corrected not only musical mistakes but also any vocal weakness or carelessness that might slip in in the ardor of singing.

Incidentally I gave singing lessons too, to earn a little

77

pocket money, and had always two or three pupils for whom I got a mark a lesson.

But the first fee in my life was earned, strangely enough, not by singing but by writing: from my childhood I had scribbled away in my spare time at poems, short stories and fairy tales—all of them sentimental.

But I simply felt that I was a writer and often sent my manuscripts to daily papers. And would you believe it, the Berlin *Tag* once printed a poem that had turned out quite nicely and I received my first fee of ten marks. This postal order which I held in hands that trembled with joy made me prouder, I believe, than many of my later fees. . . .

Mallinger was all against any waste of time.

"Off you go, my child, you can take engagements now! You must start singing to agents. I'll 'phone and make appointments for you."

I have most frightful memories of those interviews with agents: the long waiting with so many others among whom I sat, young, shy, nervous and suffering many a scornful and impertinent glance. And then the agent—oh what a mighty man was he! And so bored with everything!

"You've never been on the stage? How many rôles have you studied? Good, you'll hear from me."

Then I was outside again, dispirited and discouraged.

Mallinger would scold me.

"Don't always stand there like a silly little goose. You must give yourself airs, it's most important with those people.

You must be a little self-possessed! Where were you born? In Perleberg? Very well. But thank Heaven we're in Berlin now. You must look as if you were someone if you're to be a success."

But she was talking to deaf ears. I have never been able to put on airs.

So the auditions were always fruitless. I wrote a very depressed letter about it to Baroness Putlitz and in reply got a letter of recommendation from the Baron to one of the big agents. It was all quite different when I came with a letter like that.

Suddenly they had time for me, listened more carefully and even praised me a little . . . but it still didn't lead to any contract.

Then I had a few lessons with Herr Dahn, the stage manager of the Court Opera, to give me some idea of stage deportment. I was very clumsy, and wrung many a sigh from my patient and conscientious teacher. I studied Agathe with him. My spirits sank considerably. Would I ever learn to sing all that without constraint? to speak it as it should be spoken? I was horribly self-conscious. And even though at the elocution class in the Hochschule I could read the most tragic poem with great expression, that was quite different. There I had the book in my hand as a wall of defense to hide behind, here I stood helpless in an empty space and suddenly had two arms too many and two legs getting in my way.

I didn't know yet that the greatest and most enviable

79

thing in an actor's profession is the faculty of forgetting himself entirely, of utterly losing himself in the part he has to play, of giving up his every-day self for the wonderful illusion of some strange destiny which, in the moment of living it, becomes his own, for weal or for woe. It took me a long time before I found the way to this revelation. The best teacher of all is life. One must have experienced one's own heights and depths to become a great artist, to portray real flesh and blood. Stage experience, so frequently overestimated by the lay mind, is only the outer garment. But the pulse-beat of a rôle can only be felt by one whose own heartbeat has been quickened by sorrow and joy, sin and atonement. Only from life can life be born.

During holiday time, Frau Mallinger would have nothing to do with teaching, so I divided this holiday between my beloved Hiddensee and an invitation to Schloss Gross-Pankow, which I accepted with a beating heart. For I felt so profoundly indebted to the people who had reopened the way to my happiness that I was in constant fear lest through some clumsiness I might arouse their displeasure and make them believe that I was not sufficiently grateful. It was a long time before I learned to overcome a certain inner constraint.

The whole milieu of the castle was again quite new to me. There was, I believe, no better housekeeper than Baroness Putlitz. The whole day was mapped out, and who would not have gladly submitted to the dear maternal severity of those eyes? Oh how good this precise division of time was for me,

80

slightly spoiled by an overindulgent mother and generally arranging things as I thought good. But here it was 7 A.M., Morning Prayers. Everyone, including the entire staff of servants, had to be assembled punctually to the minute. Those summer weeks, followed later by others every year, made me an early riser, for it was a very bad thing indeed to come in late! The look the contrite sinner got prevented him from repeating it ever again. . . .

I have it all in affectionate remembrance: the sparrows chattering noisily outside in the thick rosebushes that completely covered the tower of the lovely old castle, the shafts of sunlight falling on the Bible the Baroness read from, the words of the Lord's Prayer rising from many bowed heads—and then we would seat ourselves at the long breakfast table spread invitingly with delicious fresh milk, fragrant country bread and ham. Erika and Elisabeth, the two fair daughters, and I had always some secret: we would have an eating competition, for example, and it was surprising how quickly Erika's white teeth could cope with the crusty black country bread. Soon the Baron would notice what we were doing and join in heartily. But we beat him, all three of us—he couldn't go on and was laughingly compelled to give up. Then the Baroness would put an end to this unhealthy nonsense, as she called it. And then came the morning's tasks: when the weather was good we had to work in the garden, pull up weeds, pick currants, fetch flowers for vases and strip lavender which was then put in linen bags and perfumed every

81

cupboard. When it was wet there was always sewing on the veranda. A word of praise would make me very proud, and I would brandish the darned damask table napkin like a trophy of victory. But again how shaming it was when the Baroness with a reproving look picked up some discarded cotton and carefully used it up to the last little shred. It made me blush a fiery red if the Baron was a smiling witness of this silent educational lesson. I looked up to him with enthusiastic ardor. He was goodness personified. Always a little vague and absent-minded—for he had a poet's nature—he had found the perfect complement to himself in his wife, whose correct, unsentimental, genuine sincerity compelled him to ever new admiration. It was a rarely harmonious marriage, based on the most loving understanding. I was only slightly acquainted with the three sons, who were no longer at Gross-Pankow, but with Erika, who was about my own age, I soon struck up a friendship, while Elisabeth, a few years younger, was always considered by us as rather "a child."

Erika was a happy combination of her father's clear mind and her mother's correct efficiency. To be sure there were no dreams in her blue Putlitz eyes; she laid hold of everything with firm hands and clear look—wherever life set her she would keep her place. Young though she was, people already subordinated themselves to her gladly and as a matter of course. She was always best at our tasks, and more than once she laughingly bent back the branches of a currant bush. that I had "picked bare" and collected at least another half-liter of the delicious berries that sought in vain to elude her probing eyes.

After our work in the garden we would go off swimming in one of their lumbering old coaches, each of us clapping on one of the frightful old straw hats that hung in dozens in the cloakroom—broad-brimmed and devoid of trimming. But our young faces needed no trimmings. After our bath, we would lie on the sweet-smelling meadow and my long hair that I had always been so proud of was a miserable rat's-tail compared to Erika's blonde mantle sparkling silver in the sun.

In the afternoons we would drive through the fields with the Baron himself at the reins, and it was the greatest honor to be allowed to sit beside him on the driver's seat and be put through a thorough cross-examination.

"What are those?"

"Oats."

"Wrong: barley. You'll never learn, I'm afraid. You'll only be able to sing. You'll never know anything about the cultivation and uses of lupines, but you'll always go into raptures over the sweet perfume of their lovely yellow flowers, won't you?"

"Perhaps Lotte will soon be all perfumed herself," Erika prophesied. "She will powder the nose that shines in the sun today and will go rustling about in silk petticoats."

The Baroness cast me a look of motherly solicitude.

83

"Thank Heaven she won't get very high fees to start with. So that will cut out any rustling for a while," she said vigorously. I laughed and promised neither to rustle nor to use perfume or powder.

I also sang again to the Stuttgart director who lived in summer on the neighboring estate of Retzien. The entire Putlitz family shared my excitement and joy when I was awarded the highest praise. I was carefully wrapped up in thick shawls on our drive back at night in the open carriage—they thought I was overheated after singing—and there I sat radiantly on the hard carriage seat, surrounded by attentions and good wishes like a little prima donna, and drove through the lovely summer night.

"Perhaps you will be a star in the artistic firmament one day," said the Baron, as he followed my gaze which was fixed on the shining lights of Heaven.

"A star! Oh I don't think so, Baron," I protested laughing, "I don't aspire so high. I shall be happy and contented if I get a good position in some nice, fairly good Court Theater and can sing lovely parts—in Schwerin, for example or perhaps even in Stuttgart. I think that would be marvelous." And then the true official's daughter added: "And there I'd be entitled to a pension too."

I won great praise for such solid and sensible ambitions—only the Baron didn't quite agree. His plans for me soared higher.

A few days later I was able to send home this radiant letter:

"My dear parents and Fritz,

"I've been engaged to go to Stuttgart in September!!!

"Of course it's only on a year's trial and at 150 marks a month, but I'm very happy. I won't be much called upon during the year, it will be regarded as an apprentice-year for me to get accustomed to things and go on learning a great deal. But I must tell you all about it. Yesterday at the tennis party at Retzien our Baron called me aside and said— his eyes laughing with joy: 'I am delighted to inform you that my brother is going to engage you. At present it must remain a strict secret, he desires this urgently for several reasons.' (So don't tell anybody about it. Not a word!) Then he went on: 'Go on studying until September, don't worry about money, I'll manage everything.' When I tried to thank him he put me off by saying jokingly: 'Now no sentimental fuss!' I am so very grateful to him. He was really glad and the Baroness was quite enthusiastic with pleasure. She will go on supporting me, I don't need to bother about party clothes, etc., she's seeing to that. For 100 marks I'll get full board and lodging in Stuttgart, she says, so I'll have 50 marks for myself. It's quite enough and I'll manage all right on it. I'm only terribly sorry that I can't pay you anything in the meantime and so give you some material proof of the gratitude I owe you. But it can't be helped. Everything is difficult at the start. But this year will soon be over. I said to the Baroness that the others always mentioned 300 marks. Her answer to that was that none of them were respectable, there was always something immoral mixed up in them. For a year one must be content with little, and considering I am not to be called on much, it is really quite enough. She will subsidize me so that I shall never have to call on you for assistance. She is also going to consult Fräulein von Gersdorff about my clothes. She has already spoken to Frau von Saldern who knows another lady at court. I shall stay here until the beginning of September. They are such fine people—you have no idea. The Baroness says that the Director's wife liked me very much and I shall be asked round to the family in Stuttgart. So morally I am completely assured: in everything I shall have the support of the Director and his family. I don't know yet when the contract is to be signed—I shall hear all details later. Actually he mustn't know that I know about it already as he doesn't want it to be made public, because it's a very exceptional thing to be engaged a year before. The Baron told me just because he knows how much I suffer from this uncertainty. He is so frightfully kind. I am glad I have a definite aim before me—that I can already say, I'm provided for. Only it's terrible that I can't help you. Perhaps I could give you 10 marks, 40 marks is sure to be enough pocket-money, if I have food and drink already. Then I should like to have a tea urn (we have one haven't we) so that I can sometimes

86

boil up milk for myself. I feel so peaceful and happy. Aren't you glad too? Don't worry that it's only 150 marks, it's really a great deal. What the others said was just lies. They never show you the contract either. Write soon to

"Your Lotte."

But the Baron wasn't quite happy over this Stuttgart prospect.

"Now don't think that it's all going to be quite simple for you, particularly because you have our blessing, and my brother will take an interest in you! He will always have to be careful not to show any favoritism to you as his protégée, so to speak—you can imagine what ill-feeling that could cause in the company. So, purely for the sake of fairness, you will be in danger of not getting on so well there as you might elsewhere. I am certainly glad that your desire to get an engagement is to be fulfilled. Stuttgart is a certainty. Nevertheless I should like to look about for something else."

I knew that anything the Baron did for me would be right.

He wrote to Herr Harder, the proprietor of a large agency of good repute, and I sang to him again after the holidays. The kindly old gentleman promised me his help, and he was in touch with the smaller Court theaters which were my only dream. My stage instructor, Herr Dahn, also made efforts for me. But one prospect after another fell through.

87

Suddenly a communication from Herr Dahn burst like a bomb in our good bourgeois home: I was to go to Bucharest! Thus suddenly advanced to the status of world-tourer, I sat with glowing cheeks and wrote to the Baron, while parental anxiety and fraternal fears were given vent to in hour-long consultations.

I simply could not understand why my people didn't join in my jubilation and why they had so many objections. Bucharest! Good Heavens! The silly child wanted to go all that way! Unprotected—alone, a stranger among strange people! Fritz paced up and down the room with threatening looks as though he already saw me in terrible danger. Mother wept and threw up her hands at my wanting to go to such far distant lands. Father ran from Herr Dahn to Frau Mallinger, from Frau Mallinger to Director Halpern, from Halpern to von Strauss, the Court conductor.

He came back from his visit to Herr von Strauss in great excitement. The conductor, although he thought the engagement was a good one, had on the whole shown no great enthusiasm. Indeed, when Father asked him on his honor, whether as a father he would give his consent, he answered with a decided negative. A wave of relief went through the home. Mother burst into tears of joy out of sheer relief. None of my protests made any difference. I wasn't allowed to sign the contract. With wrath and indignation I enumerated the alluring terms: 160 marks a month, free travel second-class (this specially impressed the "world-tourer" who hitherto had always traveled third-class) and twenty-five kilograms free luggage. . . .

It was no use. The brilliant offer remained in the writing desk without Father's signature.

It was only when, a few short weeks later, I read that the Halpern operatic enterprise at Sofia had come to an end owing to financial difficulties, that I realized what a good thing it was that I, an inexperienced young girl, had not been involved in this unfortunate affair.

Shortly before holidays began Herr Harder secured a contract for me with the Hamburg Municipal Theater. I signed up for three years at a monthly salary of 200 marks, rising 100 marks annually. And now the world lay before my eager feet; life, beautiful, alluring life.

But my dear careful parents wouldn't let me go alone: Father retired on a pension and it was decided that we should move to Hamburg. The world of the stage lay before me like a battlefield full of threatening dangers and unknown enemies, and my parents wanted to be loyally by my side.

Proud and happy I went off to spend my holidays at Gross-Pankow, and again passed lovely untroubled weeks with my kind friends.

I returned home with my wardrobe richly replenished, indeed with the first evening dress I had ever had in my life, a pretty white chiffon frock that seemed distractingly elegant to me and already presaged the future rustling of silk. . . .

Warm wishes accompanied my departure and a real tear glistened in the Baron's eye as he said at parting: "Remain just as you are."

Full of gratitude I said farewell from the windows of the little local train to the wide waving fields, the dark pinewood, and the huge old trees behind which lay hidden, I knew, the lovely old castle where they were thinking affectionately of me and wishing me well.

And then I stood at home again in the midst of our red plush furniture and Mother was stretching out happy arms and Father's eyes were twinkling at me and Fritz was bidding me a glad welcome—and no castle in all the world was so dear and lovely to me as that familiar room, those old-fashioned bourgeois surroundings. It was my real "home." And that is the loveliest word of all.

And this "home" I took with me to Hamburg into the strange new world of the theater. Fritz had to stay in Berlin. And I took with me more ambitious thoughts than I had ever yet cherished. . . .

So I set off for Hamburg full of expectation; and as the wonderful old Hanseatic city came into view all my love and delight went out to it at first sight, as they still do whenever I stand by the green banks of the Alster, or view the magnificent panorama of the harbor. . . .

CHAPTER
EIGHT

WE HAD found a very pretty flat in the Ilse Strasse. From our covered balcony we looked out on to swaying treetops, the Alster was very near—and where are there lovelier walks than along the Alster promenade, past lovely villas with well-kept gardens, bright flower beds, and big lawns reminiscent of England. On the very first evening I ran off to the Alster just to snatch a glimpse of the lovely scene. But the next afternoon I went to the theater. I took with my signed contract a letter addressed to the director, Councillor Bachur, in which I thanked him for the engagement and promised to show myself worthy of his trust by my great assiduity. He must have been somewhat surprised at this naïve declaration, but, in any case, he received me very kindly and said that Baron Putlitz and also Frau Mallinger had written to him, and he would pay special attention to me. Then I was dismissed and gave a sigh of relief, for all my aunts and uncles in Berlin had described the director of a theater to me as a regular bogeyman. They were all of them cunning seducers, and any good part must be paid for promptly with so-called love. . . . So I had gone into the director's room with the fixed determination to hit out at him at any attempt at seduction. Fortunately my bellicose attitude vanished the moment I stood before the little, gray-haired councillor, who, after one absent-minded look of fatherly benevolence from his sharp eyeglasses, dismissed me hastily. Oh Heavens, this was no seducer . . . my virtue seemed assured. . . .

At that time Gustav Brecher was the quite exceptional first conductor at the Hamburg Theater. Otto Klemperer came at the same time as I did and created a great sensation. I found him enormously interesting, this thin young man as tall as a lamppost with the mournful, burning eyes and pale cheeks. I invested him with romantic glamour and had quite a passion for him, whereas Brecher seemed almost godlike in his remote supremacy, and a friendly smile from him would throw me into a state of nervous confusion. I had sung to them both, had earned their friendly praise and now was given a part—that of the Third Boy in the *Magic Flute*. The First Boy was called Magda Lohse, the Second, Anne-marie Birkenström. I was soon fast friends with the two of them and we still keep in touch today; and when Magda, now married in Stuttgart, came to see me in some town near by during one of my tours, we had such endless things to say about those early days that it was daybreak before we could tear ourselves away and I remember that I had a big concert to give. . . .

I was also given the part of Valkyrie, Gerhide, and it was this part I had to sing at my first rehearsal. Felix Landau, the coach, a stout little man, sat at the piano in a very bad temper and looked crossly at me.

"Never been in a theater, eh?" was how he greeted me. "No notion of Gerhide, eh what? Probably no rhythm either, eh?" Full of shame I had to admit to all three charges. And with a daring "Hojotoho" I made my first leap into the new life.

Felix Landau regarded me much more benevolently. "You've a very nice voice. I'll recommend you for Bayreuth."

Oh how my heart beat with rapture! I had no idea, of course, that the good Felix distributed his favors promiscuously and en masse. . . . He was a fine musician, but an excessively naïve person, the butt of every jest, the credulous victim of every conceivable stupid trick. The great respect I felt for him lasted just as long as this first rehearsal. Later, like everyone else, I learned not to take him seriously. But if I needed to practice at something really thoroughly and urgently, I would just have to say: "Felix, no one can play like you. You're the greatest genius I know. Please coach me thoroughly in this—no one else can."

Then his dear old face would be transfigured by a radiant smile, and I could be sure that I wouldn't leave the rehearsal without having mastered what I had set out to do.

I remember with horror my first stage rehearsal. As the *Magic Flute* was already on the repertoire, it was really decidedly lucky for me that there was a rehearsal with orchestra at all. But there were several new people in the principal parts, so the scenes with the Three Boys were rehearsed too. Magda and Annemarie had already been a year in the theater and helped to cheer me up, for I felt like dying with fright. The palm branch wobbled precariously in my hand as we came on, and unfortunately my looks of misery awakened no feelings of sympathy in the producer. "Why do you look as if you were at a funeral?" he shouted nastily at me.

"Well, it's the first time I've ever sung with an orchestra," I whispered back in a voice choked with tears of anguish.

"Well what about it! That's no reason! You're supposed to be charming boys, smiling and gay, not mourners at a funeral."

I tried to be charming, smiling and gay. . . . But it was a miserable failure, for I had to watch what I was singing.

"How is it humanly possible to think of everything at once?" I kept thinking! I felt a complete failure, and would have liked to run away from the whole thing.

But even a rehearsal must come to an end sometime.

The day of the performance approached and a pair of buskins had to be bought, for shoes and stockings were not provided. The buskins were dear and Father looked cross. I also had to get a tin box to hold my grease paints, and then came the exciting business of making-up. Armed with colored pencils, powder puffs and hares'-feet, I sat quite helplessly at the mirror that reflected my sun-burned girlish face. Oh

Heavens! And I was supposed to be a "gay boy" this evening.... I peeped cautiously across at Annemarie with whom
I shared a dressing room. She was working away at her
face like an Indian preparing for the war dance. I watched
the transformation in amazement! Under her command I
started doing my own face, but she was quick-tempered and
grew very cross at my inefficiency. Nevertheless I thought I
looked simply marvelous with my satanically blackened eyes,
red lips and boldly outlined eyebrows. Then I put on the
rather tattered curly blond wig, and curtseyed laughingly to
the strange, incredibly altered face in the mirror that was
supposed to be mine. And only then came the costume!
Blue tights and a white tunic which, pull at it as I might,
wouldn't cover as much of me as I wanted. . . . I felt terribly
shy as we came down the steep stairs and stood among a great
crowd of people, soloists, chorus, supers, ballet-dancers and
stage hands. . . . Actually, of course, nobody paid any attention to me. But in my embarrassment I got a proper per-
secution mania and felt that all eyes were upon me. My tunic
started splitting at every seam, I kept pulling at it so. Anxiously shielding myself with my palm branch I fled into the
darkest wings. But the callboy shouted to me that we must
get ready and Annemarie muttered to me: "Now be quiet.
You'll send us off our heads with your nerves. Why on
earth did you go on the stage?" And we stepped forward
into the cruel glare of the footlights. Behind this blinding
and irritating strip of light I at first saw only the gleam of

Brecher's very white cuffs, then the orchestra, and then, beyond—the enemy, the audience. And yet my fear didn't even get as far. It stopped at the bright head of the conductor down below. Just like a schoolgirl saying her piece, her only anxiety being to please the teacher, so I sang my part. If only I could please Brecher! That was the principal thing. Beyond, the enemy was warded off by the slim black form at the conductor's desk, his eyeglasses flashing threateningly in the bright light, his waving hands seeming to draw out our melody in an amazingly flattering way, until my voice like a fluttering bird settled on them and gradually began consciously to hover and wing farther into the huge wide semi-darkness of the theater. When we had gone off I wiped the drops of anguish from my brow. But I was pleased and happy that everything had gone so well.

Then came all the little parts that every beginner is so mortified at having to do: Pages in *Tannhäuser* and *Lohengrin,* Apprentices in the *Meistersinger,* Bridesmaids in the *Freischütz.* But however much the other three Pages stormed and raged, I was quite pleased not to have a part that might involve the terrifying experience of having to cross the entire stage alone. How one would ever get across without stumbling was beyond me! . . .

"It's a scandal that we've got to sing the Pages," said Annemarie. "You've no stage blood in you, Lotte, if you're always thinking: I couldn't do that. You'll never have a career that way. You're always frightened of not being able to do something."

"The Third Page in *Tannhäuser* is so difficult," I wailed, "it's so hard to get that F-sharp. Your parts are all much easier. You watch, I'll miss it this evening."

And miss it I did.

"Wolfram von Eschenbach, beginne" was a discord—and what a furious look Brecher gave me.

"Give that part to someone else," he declared categorically.

It was my first painful experience at the theater. I wept bitter tears. Annemarie comforted me:

"You should be very glad," she said, "that you've got out of that silly Page's part. It's the sort of part that can stick to you for years. Brecher will soon forget that you went wrong—and you needn't sing it any longer."

But I wanted to sing it. . . . I wanted to sing absolutely anything just to learn not to regard the stage as foreign territory. So I waited for Brecher outside the rehearsal room and when he came out I burst into tears and begged him to give me back my Page's part. He looked surprised and amused. It was certainly the first time a soloist had ever begged for that little part that everyone is glad not to have to sing.

"Very well," he said, keeping a straight face with difficulty, "if you promise never to sing a wrong note again, I shall let mercy temper justice."

And I rushed off happily.

A short time after, I got my first really nice part, that of Anna in the *Merry Wives*.

A duet—and an aria!

I learned with tremendous zeal, for I had been promised that I should sing at the Sunday matinee. The chorus master, Harmans, conducted. He coached me thoroughly and kindly and henceforth became the guardian angel of my novitiate. I could always ask his advice—and it was always good advice. To me he was a good and unselfish friend.

Brecher praised me highly; he had listened to my first big venture and afterward came on the stage. I stood there beaming as I had never beamed before, dazed and confused with the first applause I had ever had of my very own, after my aria. Brecher clapped me kindly on the back.

"Just keep it up," he said with a smile, and his clever eyes gave me a benevolent look through his shining glasses. "I've already got a reward for you: the lovely part of Sophie in Strauss's new opera *Rosenkavalier*. It would be a marvelous chance for you."

I could scarcely stammer out my thanks—from sheer happiness.

When I got the part from Schach, the librarian, I was amazed at the great task that Brecher had entrusted to an untried person like me. I studied it with fanatical zeal, and it was a bitter disappointment to me when I didn't sing it on the first night Elisabeth Schumann, already one year in the theater and a great favorite: in Hamburg with considerable

As the Marschallin in Strauss's *Rosenkavalier*.

and honorable successes to her credit, sang at the first performance by special request of Edyth Walker, the Octavian.
Brecher, too, was speedily won over to Schumann, who as
well as singing enchantingly was also a clever and graceful
actress already and didn't give Jelenko, the producer, as
much trouble as I, suffering as I did from terrible inhibitions
and being hopelessly self-conscious on the stage. At the
time, of course, I thought it an atrocious injustice that I
hadn't been allowed to do the first performance. I regarded
Elisabeth as the world's greatest intriguer—a rôle which,
Heaven knows, was quite foreign to her nature—and felt
myself misunderstood and ousted from my rightful place.
Resentfully I sat in the stalls, a member of the second cast,
and Brecher's kindly consolation that I would soon be singing the nice part—a bit later, of course, but quite definitely—
filled me with wrath and powerless protest. Elisabeth, always a good colleague, was well aware of my unjustified
mistrust. She took great pains to be especially nice to me, but
all the precepts of all my friends and relations at which I
had once laughed and now mistakenly found true, recurred
to me: "All colleagues are bad. They're all your enemies. . . ."

Incidentally one will scarcely anywhere find nicer or more
helpful comrades than on the stage. The legends of the
intrigues of malicious colleagues are just inventions of the unsuccessful. In general we feel like comrades-in-arms—and
who would betray his friend on the field of battle? The few
that really do are branded for us with the mark of Cain,

they have no real friends and are "outsiders," expelled from the band of true comrades. . . .

My desire to be given parts was awakened the first time I had won genuine applause. I now became a real nuisance to the directorate. I stood at every door waiting to pluck any of the "chiefs" by their coattails and plead with them for a new rôle.

The good old porter Haake, who from his sheltered seat had for many years looked on with philosophic calm at the mad proceedings, and past whom had raged the hysterical screams of mortified prima donnas, deeply-injured tenors and snorting producers, leaving him quite unmoved, was my special friend. Enthroned in his lodge, fat and always peacefully chewing away, he was constantly and piously devoted to the strenuous business of eating, and he would watch me benevolently as I hovered uncertainly between the doors of the director and the producer.

"He's in a bad mood today," he would say, pointing with his thumb at the "directorial" door.

"What about Jelle?" (That was our name for Jelenko, the producer.)

"He's always in a temper," was the not very comforting reply. I looked anxiously into Haake's honest face with its clear kind eyes. He nodded with a smile, uncorked the milk bottle his thoughtful wife had provided him with, and first of all fortified himself thoroughly. Then he chewed away contentedly at one of the countless sandwiches whose inexhaustible supply preserved his life.

"Oh, Herr Haake," I said, "what do you think of this dirty trick: they've taken the part of Sophie in the *Rosenkavalier* away from me and given it to Schumann. Have you ever heard of anything so mean?"

"Yes," said Haake, chewing away. "Yes I have. Quite often. But you're still young. You must learn to be patient. You always want everything at once. And all this asking for parts—that won't help you. In the theater everything is just chance. You watch, you'll soon be thinking of ol' Haake: it'll be chance that will make a career for you."

"But when will this chance come?" I cried desperately. "They're all against me. Jelle says I'm too awkward—a hopeless case he calls me. He said I kept beating time on the stage all the time I was singing Anna in the *Merry Wives*. But the people *did* clap."

"But you've also got a lovely voice," said Haake. "I hear everyone talking about you. No, no one's against you, Fräulein Lehmann. And now pluck up your courage; if you want to get something out of Jelle go on in, he can't do you any harm."

So off I went, knocked at the door, and opened it as if it led to the cage of a dangerous tiger.

Chief-producer and Vice-director Jelenko turned his well-nourished red face toward me. He sat at his desk, immersed

101

in mysterious repertoire plans, casting problems and accounts. Jelle lived only for the theater, the "Institute," as he called it. For the Institute he certainly would have sold his soul to the devil. His big face, reminiscent of a cross schoolboy's grown old, made a threatening appearance wherever anything went wrong. Then would come the row—a terrific thunderstorm would break loose. To me Jelle was the personification of the word "row," so it is not incomprehensible that I stood in the doorway with a beating heart. . . .

"What's the matter? Why are you bothering me again?" he growled disagreeably.

"Herr Jelenko, please," I stammered, "please—when am I going to sing Sophie? When does the second cast come on?"

"When it's put on," was the oracular reply. Jelle brought out a huge colored handkerchief and blew his nose at great length, with much noise and abandon. He still looked grim and angry. I didn't understand his ways, so was terrified of him and would certainly have doubted the sanity of anyone who had predicted that this angry man whose bushy gray hair always seemed to be bristling with rage, would one day be a great friend of mine, and in later years would be identified with the friendly memory of the Hamburg Municipal Theater—and the red full moon of his face, perpetually shining with zeal, wrath or uncontrolled mirth, would become familiar and dear to me. . . .

"You're to learn Freya's part in *Rheingold*," said Jelle, his

102

voice emerging from the depths of his enormous handkerchief. "Arthur Nikisch is conducting—and you, Heaven help us, are going to be Freya."

Even the "Heaven help us" didn't detract from my joy. . . . Ecstatically I rushed past Haake's lodge shouting to him: "I'm going to sing Freya." He chewed away delightedly.

Then I learned that his prophecy had come true: the singer originally intended to do Freya's part had fallen ill, and I was taking her place. Chance had helped me. . . .

I had soon learned the part—and then came the rehearsal, an orchestral one right away, with Nikisch. As I appeared high up among the crags, my anguished cry for help was really quite genuine. But it was probably more realistic than musically accurate. . . . Nikisch rapped on the desk and said with the charm and enchanting amiability of which only he was capable: "Would you mind coming down from your mountain tops, please. Yes—here. Right up to the footlights! You're a beginner, I hear. But you mustn't be so terribly frightened. Just take a good look at me. Do I look as bad as all that? Well then, let's try again."

Ah, if only everyone spoke as kindly to a terrified little beginner! It would be so much easier!

It suddenly went well; the kindly nod from the desk, the encouraging smile—oh, how they cheered me up!

Proud and delighted, I looked at my reflection on the evening: I rather liked myself as a goddess with sprays of blossom in my fair hair and flowing robes. . . . Nikisch praised

103

me, everyone was nice and kind—so I sent a triumphant telegram to my anxious brother waiting in Berlin saying "great success."

It was slightly premature and slightly over optimistic. The press unfortunately did not share my enthusiasm for myself.

The *Hamburger Fremdenblatt,* for instance, wrote:

"A Fräulein Lehmann sang and played the part of Freya with touching ungainliness. As to the vocal qualities of the young lady, whose throat seemed constricted by excessive nervousness, we can as yet say nothing."

Another paper found that I was "quite miscast" and while one did at least allow that I looked nice, "which incidentally did not make up for her lack of vocal and histrionic talent," one particularly severe-minded critic thought that among the gods of Valhalla I had looked more like a nice little domestic kitten than an august goddess. This "domestic kitten" particularly enraged me as I thought of the flowing gown, whose treacherous folds it had been a real achievement not to trip over . . . and of the wreath of flowers in my blonde curls— and was very pleased with my critical inspection. Long indignant letters of complaint went forth into the world—but no one took this failure as tragically as I. Not even Director Bachur. I was given very nice parts to sing, Irene in *Rienzi,* Gutrune, Sophie (with good notices), May in *Heimchen am Herd (The Cricket on the Hearth).* Elisabeth Schumann was a charming Heimchen. I still see her attractive face with the black cherry eyes laughing under the gray, peaked cap. I

104

didn't feel like laughing. I felt so clumsy among all those clever actors round about me! Katharina Fleischer-Edel, shyly adored, when playing the part of Dot, would often whisper to me on the stage: "Don't be frightened—act more freely. . . ." But how could I help being frightened when in the second act Max Lohfing, who was always given to practical joking, and Bobby vom Scheidt slowly started tying me up for fun with a ball of wool and waited with mischievous faces for the moment when I had to stand up. Helplessly I gazed down on the strands of wool that bound me to my seat, while Elisabeth, the kindly Heimchen, made desperate signals to me from the wings to break them, as tears of laughter rolled down her cheeks. Those were terrible moments when I felt with anguish how clumsy and lacking in presence of mind I was.

In Altona I often sang Agathe. We moved over into the "suburbs" like a traveling troupe with our make-up boxes under our arms; twice a week they had opera and the rest of the time plays—both theaters were managed by the same directorate. Unfortunately no one ever took Altona really seriously, and an opera with Max Lohfing, Bobby vom Scheidt and Eduard Lichtenstein in it together was just a joy to us all. Every word of the dialogue would be distorted. If the libretto read: "He has made it warm for me," Bobby vom Scheidt would be sure to move his arms about like a frozen cabby and shriek through the Wolf-glen: "It's very cold here!"

105

When I saw the same artists in serious parts that demanded their full concentration, I could scarcely believe they were the same people. . . . How warmheartedly and with what simple humanity Lohfing sang Rocco—how incomparable he was as Falstaff! What a magnificent Sachs Bobby vom Scheidt made!

I was profoundly stirred on evenings when Elisabeth was sung with all the spiritual purity of Fleischer-Edel's voice, or when Walker was a wonderful Brünhilde or a sublime Isolde.

Unforgettable was that darling of the gods—Caruso. I first heard him as Don José. Thrilling as an actor, quite apart from his singing, he was a revelation to me. Trembling with emotion I followed the destiny that was being enacted before me with overpowering realism. His complete abandonment to his part communicated itself to his audience, breathless under the spell, and I am sure that many who had only come "because one must have been there" forgot about sensation and remembered only Caruso.

I had studied Eurydice for the second presentation, and had the great joy of having to sing it on a Caruso evening. After our *Orpheus* he was to sing *Pagliacci*, and as he always dressed very early he stood in the wings nearly all the time and listened to Metzger's wonderful Orpheus and my Eurydice. What a thrill it was when he came up to me in the wings after the performance and cried, wringing my hand: "*Ah, brava, brava! Che bella magnifica voce! Una voce*

106

Italiana!" Quite dazed with joy I rushed off to my dressing room and—wonder of wonders—Jelenko came in, said a few kind words and delivered an invitation from Councillor Bachur to a dinner *en petit comité* in honor of Caruso. I stared speechlessly at Jelle's red face which today looked less grim. Why had I been thus honored—I among all the other members of the cast? "It was Caruso himself that wanted you to come too," Jelle added, retreating behind his inevitable handkerchief.

"Caruso wanted me to come," I thought agitatedly while I stood in the wings during *Pagliacci* watching and listening to him with all my eyes and ears. . . . I choked for breath when he tore off the clown's cap with a wild gesture and wiped the paint from his face and sang: *"Non sono piu pagliaccio."* Tears ran down his face and at the end of the performance he was exhausted to the point of collapse.

The miracle of this great grace of getting away from yourself and being another person, of being reborn—for hours shaping another strange destiny—and then of emerging unscathed from the whirling vortex of vivid experience into a calmer existence: all this was revealed to me more powerfully, more stirringly than ever before.

I felt that I would find the way to this grace—in spite of all obstacles.

The next evening I sat next to Caruso at table. But unfortunately we didn't have much conversation: my school French and English dried up from sheer nervousness, my

Italian was limited to a few texts of songs, and Caruso did not speak a word of German. So it was translated to me that he thought my voice was charming and would like to have me as a colleague the next day to sing Micæla. My pleading glances at Jelenko, however were ignored.

"Impossible, she has never sung Micæla!" was his decision, delivered in his own peculiar irascible way. At that moment I hated him. Under the table Caruso pulled at my scarf to show his sympathy. . . . I sat there with burning cheeks. . . .

The next day I received a telegram from his secretary: Signor Commendatore Enrico Caruso invited me to have supper with him at his hotel after the *Carmen* performance. I sat with the wire before me, frozen stiff with terror.

I was just a great baby and imagined that temptation had come to me in the guise of the loveliest voice in the world. . . . So I fetched my French dictionary and wrote a polite refusal. Quickly, before I could regret it, I took it round myself to the hotel. On the way there I passed the theater and heard Hindermann saying to Fleischer-Edel: "Will you be at Caruso's after the performance tonight?" I stopped and asked whether Caruso was giving a party today. Yes! an enormous dinner at his hotel. . . . Oh what luck that I had found out in time! So it was not for me alone—my dark yet dangerously alluring presentiments of a *chambre séparée* were quite unjustified. My letter of refusal fluttered to the ground in little pieces!

108

In the evening I sat opposite Caruso at table, but he was exhausted and monosyllabic, his eyes weary. With a shy request for his autograph I passed a picture postcard of him across the table. He gave me a friendly look, just having realized who I was, wrote my address on the card and put it in his pocket. With rapid strokes he substituted a caricature of himself on the back of the menu card.

The next day I received a huge lovely photograph of him with the following dedication: *"À Mademoiselle Lotte Lehmann, la charmante et jolie Eurydike, très sincèrement— Enrico Caruso."*

But the favoritism I enjoyed while he was there was quite fleeting and had no aftereffects. I was nothing more than one of the four pages who made way for Elsa of Brabant, and invited Wolfram von Eschenbach to sing—apprentices who made merry in Acts I and II of the *Meistersinger* and filled in the long wait before the Field of Song by rolling up our coats under our heads and pitching a camp on the floor of the big communal greenroom—much to the wrath of the severe wardrobe mistress, Hulda Wolf, who applied her masterful methods with the department of theatrical tailoring to us beginners as well. We were literally in terror of her—and every evening when I came to be dressed, the first question I used to ask the nice young blonde dresser was always: "Is Hulda in a good temper?" . . .

At the close of my first opera season, Councillor Bachur retired and Brecher and Edyth Walker left Hamburg. I was sorry to lose Brecher. He was always kind to me, helped me whenever he could, and I learned a great deal from him. A part studied with him remained firmly anchored in one's mind. The complete realization of a musical phrase was what he revealed to me. Like a connoisseur he would mold every word in the music, and under his hands everything became amazingly clear and clean. Many people could not follow his very personal, almost dancing way of conducting. I could understand it very well and found it almost difficult later to get accustomed to a quieter conducting technique. When, years later, I had again the pleasure of cooperating with Brecher, I felt with the old rapture how my voice floated from those nervous, dancing hands, just as it used to—and everything to me was clear and simple that may perhaps have seemed unusual and complicated to many.

The new director, Dr. Hans Loewenfeld, whose fame as a marvelous producer had preceded him, opened the season with a magnificent performance of *Aïda*, conducted by Felix von Weingartner, who had come to us as first conductor. Lucille Marcelle, his wife, was Aïda, exotic and seductive, with a deep velvety voice, a southern flower transplanted to the northern cold of Hamburg. . . .

Weingartner was very interested in my voice which he thought very beautiful, but he lived artistically only for his adored wife, and was—how can I express it—so "remote" that I could scarcely hope for any real promotion from him. In spite of my little successes I was of absolutely no account

110

in the theater—just one of the "four." Annemarie Birkenstrom, Magda Lohse and Grete Schlegel, the other three, hadn't even sung so many "big" parts as I had, and said I was conceited not to be satisfied.

But one person who clung obstinately to the hope that I might get somewhere was the conductor, Otto Klemperer. He also specially drew the attention of Dr. Loewenfeld to me. Loewenfeld, however, had brought a whole staff of new singers with him who had to be placed first of all—and many of whom soon vanished into obscurity.

Once I had an opportunity of singing a few arias to him in private, in the house of Max Loewengard, the critic of the *Hamburg Correspondent*. I was a great friend of his two daughters, Cilly and Leisel, and Loewengard thought highly of my voice and predicted for me a great future, which I believed in least of all. So there the new director listened to me attentively, regarded me with increased interest, extended my contract on the spot with proportional increase and again promised me a very good part very shortly. A few days later I was given the part of Martha in the *Evangelimann*. Now this is a rôle that demands a certain amount of acting experience. To fill in the long musical interlude by good acting was no easy task for me, blessed as I was with warmth and sensibility, but with no experience or knowledge of acting. So this attempt turned out pretty miserably—and Loewenfeld immediately lost all interest in me. He was a man of the moment, entirely without patience, loved

111

great temperaments and interesting actors, and, being a producer of genius, got the very best out of them. But he was quite incapable of awakening talent. Anything that wasn't an immediate success at the first call, he dropped like a hot coal. . . . I was now so mercilessly and unconditionally condemned that Klemperer thought it more advisable in my own interests to send in my resignation. This was a bitter blow for us all. What were we to do? My parents had moved to Hamburg with me. Should they now go back to Berlin? They couldn't lead a gypsy's life and follow me round everywhere—Mother's health was too bad for that. She still suffered terribly from gastric spasms. Our financial position had not improved either; with his pension Father had considerably less than before, and out of my pay had to come all sorts of things that weren't provided for by the theater: shoes, stockings, wigs, etc. So there were often messages of distress to my brother in Berlin—and he always managed to send money; he stinted himself in every way so as to be able to rescue us again.

And now new uncertainties were to be added to this!

Klemperer found all these worries quite unnecessary: I would be certain to get another engagement. But here there wasn't much hope for me. Loewenfeld saw absolutely no future for me, misjudged me and thought simply nothing of me. So I wrote to my agent Harder and explained my position. Harder sent me what seemed a very good contract with the Berlin Court Opera which would be confirmed after a guest performance, if they were pleased with me. Moreover there were prospects at Wiesbaden, Schwerin and Rostock. So I went to Dr. Loewenfeld and asked him to release me from my contract at the end of the season. He agreed immediately, obviously relieved at being rid of me.

In the course of long consultations with my friend Loewengard it was decided that I must go on studying. Loewenfeld was not only disappointed with my acting but also with my voice which he found beautiful but not rich. I went to that distinguished singing teacher, Alma Schadow, and with renewed intensive studies felt greater strength and brilliance flood my voice. Loewenfeld, who expected great things from those studies, proposed that I should wait a year before I went, to complete a trial year, so to speak, and then the Berlin Court Opera was in no particular hurry to have me, and would be very pleased to wait, so Harder wrote. . . .

113

CHAPTER
NINE

IT WAS then that I began to realize that an artist must never stop learning. He has never finished with his studies and always, even when he stands on heights of perfection, he needs an adviser, an observant friend whose experienced and knowledgeable ear will perceive the slightest dullness on the luster of his voice, and like a mirror will reveal to the singer not only his virtues but all the little irregularities and inaccuracies that creep in. Of course one knows singers who keep an exact control of themselves even in matters of vocal technique, and notice every deviation. But I give myself to my part with all my soul. I cannot think of technical matters while I sing, because I live what I sing so completely that there is no room left for anything else. So it is good that a new period of study, refining, refreshing and reassuring, should guide the voice back to the quiet ways of honest self-knowledge.

I studied for a long time with Frau Schadow in Hamburg and owe a great deal to her. I was also with Hedwig Francillo-Kauffmann and tried to learn the secret of her silvery agility. Katherine Fleischer-Edel also took a kindly concern in my voice. In Vienna I studied for a short time with the unforgettable Elise Elizza and Frau Professor Brossement with whom one's voice is in such very good hands. Particularly stimulating I found the chamber-music singer Frau Felicia Kaszowska. A mæstra of the old school of Jean de Reszke and Lamperti, grown great in a time whose brilliance has already become for us a proud tradition, she is well fitted to transmit her rich experiences to those who come so eagerly to learn from her. I spent many interesting and illuminating hours with her and owe her a great deal of artistic inspiration.

It does one good to cry a halt sometimes to this pursuit of perfection and success which the life of an "arrived" artist entails. . . . It does one good to reflect on the fact that perfection is still a distant goal . . . that one must be constantly beginning again—constantly building up anew!

I still see peaks before me to be conquered. There are still steep paths I must tread. And I shall say: I have got there, only when it means that I am saying farewell. . . .

So now there came a time of intensive study. I used my summer holidays, too, to accompany Frau Schadow to a watering place on a pretty inland lake, and go on studying with her there. For the next season must really mean promotion or at least far-reaching decisions and undertakings.

The next season started off just as usual—one nice part on

115

a Sunday afternoon in Altona—as makeshift for someone
else—otherwise pages and apprentices. . . .

One day Klemperer called me. I still had my old passion
for him and stood before him in some confusion.

"Do you think you could manage to take on Elsa's part?
You'd only have a week. Frau Wagner is on holiday,
Fleischer-Edel is away too at the moment—and we're in a fix.
I've persuaded Dr. Loewenfeld to let you risk it. Well—do
you think you can do it?"

Did I think I could do it!

I had, of course, studied Elsa's part by myself and came
proudly to the rehearsal. But if I thought I knew the part,
I realized my mistake after the first five minutes. Klemperer
sat at the piano like an evil spirit, thumping on it with long
hands like tigers' claws, dragging my terrified voice into the
fiery vortex of his fanatical will. Elsa's dreamy serenity became a rapturous ecstasy, her anxious pleading a challenging
demand. For the first time I felt my nervous inhibitions fall
from me, and I sank into the flame of inner experience. I
had always wanted to sing like this—it was like flying in a
dream: a bodiless gliding through blissful eternity. . . . But
usually one wakens from this lovely kind of dream with the
terror of falling. And so I was dragged back from those
ecstasies by Klemperer's voice saying: "No idea of the part.
We must work hard if you're to manage it."

I managed it.

I sang Elsa in spite of the indignant looks of Pennarini,

116

my Lohengrin, in spite of the producer's shrugged shoulders, in spite of Klemperer's discouraging interpolations at the orchestral rehearsal. . . .

Theo Drill-Orridge was singing Ortrud on a visiting engagement, and her eyes grew wider as she noticed at the rehearsal how simply everyone was against me—even Klemperer, who grew furious every time I forgot anything, seemed to lose all confidence in me and shouted up: "What's the matter? Has the big part gone to your head and made you forget everything?"

But now I set my teeth, and plunged into the hazards of this great undertaking.

I didn't see the audience—probably a skeptical one expecting nothing very special—on the evening. Nor did I see Dr. Loewenfeld's dreaded face spying from the box. . . . I was just Elsa! I felt only the blissful pulsation of my voice, I forgot everything that conductor and producer had pumped into me—I was just myself alone. Tears stood in my eyes as I passed down the minster steps through the bowing throng.

"Hail to thee, Elsa of Brabant," sang the chorus—and, "Hail to thee," my whole heart sang, greeting this day that was the real beginning of my rise to fame.

Of course that Elsa was far from being a mature artistic achievement. Probably a great deal of it was primitive and gauche, yet that evening is one of the sacred high points of my life, for whose sake life has been worth living.

117

It was a great and decisive success both with the audience and the press.

With one stroke I was "made." Naturally there was no more talk of the contract being broken, and I was signed up on very decent terms with the Hamburg Municipal Theater.

One big part after another in the dramatic soprano repertoire was mastered, and I continued to have an increasing success.

My partner in all the grand operas was principally Heinreich Hensel, now a long-established and highly successful singing master in München. When I saw him recently, we reminded each other of many battles we had gone through together. We also recalled one amusing episode. Once, when we were in the midst of taking poetic farewells in the moonlight scene in the *Evangelimann,* I missed the seat altogether and sat flat on the ground. Our laughter at my slip was so uncontrolled that the lovely melodious duet, "We sit embracing in the silver moonlight," wasn't sung at all, and the helpless conductor searched frantically for us in vain, for we were sitting in the arbor where we should have been exchanging parting vows—nearly dying with laughter. When the act was at last over, we stared disconcertedly at each other as the lights went up; thick black rivulets of tears had flowed from our carefully blackened eyelashes—and drawn deep furrows on our faces!

So many lovely voices from the Hamburg Theater pass through my mind: Karl Günther's soft, luminous tenor;

Ottilie Metzger-Lattermann's ardent, passionate contralto; the soft stream of Sabine Kalter's warm, dark voice; Anna Scheffler's triumphant soprano—they are all priceless sounds that have remained in my ears, like the cry of Drill-Orridge's "Hojotoho" and the sweet silvery violin tone of the unforgettable Fleischer-Edel, and Richard Schubert's splendid heroic portrayals. Wonderful, beautiful memories that never die!

And how happy we always were! On *Parsifal* evenings, for instance, we would already laugh ourselves hoarse while we were dressing as flower maidens: Martha Winternitz-Dorda, a sound musician and absolutely infallible, came to the rescue of many a wobbly ensemble when the overmerry flower maidens were fooling round with that gentle poetical Parsifal, Otto Marak. Marak was frequently my partner, and I shall never forget the tender quality of his gentle, spiritual voice.

CHAPTER
TEN

ONE DAY when I was to sing Michæla, I heard that Gregor, director of the Vienna Court Opera, had come to the theater to hear the tenor.

"Sing well," someone shouted to me, "and perhaps he'll engage you!"

I just laughed.

Vienna! The Vienna Court Opera! That still lay in the clouds, inaccessible—for all my nice successes. Vienna is the dream of every singer, and to me, up there in northerly Hamburg, it seemed like a star that one could not aspire to. So I sang my Micæla and smilingly received the applause thinking happily: Oh, dear Hamburg, how I love you. I just want to stay here and sing and be popular and always improve. . . .

The next day Norbert Salter, the manager, summoned me to his hotel. Theo Drill-Orridge, our interesting and very successful dramatic soprano, had previously introduced me to him with the warmest recommendations.

Salter sat at the writing desk, and I listened in amazement

to several telephone conversations in which fees of thousands were bandied about like colored balls. Then, radiating good will, Salter turned his smiling face to me and said: "I'm going to tell you a story. You know who Director Gregor is, don't you? Well, he came to Hamburg to engage a tenor and was at the *Carmen* performance yesterday. He listened very attentively to the tenor. And then, when we met after the performance, he pushed aside the contract I had already made out, and just said: 'I'm going to engage Micæla for Vienna. Lehmann is her name, isn't it? All right then.'" Salter made a dramatic pause. "And here is your contract."

I looked at him—speechless.

"Well—have you nothing to say?"

No, I had nothing to say.

I seized the pen and would have signed then and there without having read the contract at all. I saw the lengthy figure of the salary, the long term of years—did I need to think it over? Yet I did stop. I must first go to Dr. Loewenfeld and tell him about this wonderful offer. After all, it was under him that I had had my first successes, and I was now one of his most highly esteemed associates. We had also come to a complete artistic understanding during his distinguished production of *Iphigénie* conducted by Selmar Meyrowitz, Felix von Weingartner's successor. Drill-Orridge as a monumental Clytemnestra, Günther singing magnificently as Achilles, Bürs (who unfortunately died so young)

121

as a noble Agamemnon—it was a wonderful performance which caught up my Iphigénie to classic heights. . . .

Now that I had achieved my aims, I was attached to Hamburg with all my heart. And now the clarion call, "The Vienna Court Opera," had come like a challenge to my cheerful content. . . . And yet I felt strongly that the offer was too great for me not to consider seriously. My good parents wanted to go to Vienna too, but Father, so very Prussian, a German official to the core, how would he feel in lighthearted Vienna? But he wanted to come. He lived only for my voice and my career. And Mother? Whither indeed should such a good mother not follow her child? She did not ask many questions. It was enough for her that I would need her. And that meant she would come too. . . .

I took my Vienna contract first to Jelenko, with whom I had become great friends, and Jelle, who wanted to keep me at the Hamburg Opera at any cost, rushed off to Dr. Loewenfeld.

"If you give her twelve thousand marks a year, she'll stay in Hamburg."

"Twelve thousand marks! Has she become a megalomaniac? I shouldn't dream of it."

Two obstinate people at loggerheads!

Jelenko returned, scarlet with rage.

"He won't do it," he shrieked infuriatedly. "He thinks the Vienna contract is just bluff. But wait, little Lehmann, I beg you. Wait a little. He'll have to give in."

122

As Elsa in *Lohengrin*.

In Title Role of *Fidelio*.

—*Ellinger*

Jelle sank groaning into his huge colored handkerchief and I went home defiantly, to find a telegram from Salter urging an immediate decision.

So I signed the Vienna contract.

Loewenfeld still held out. Between us, in spite of our great artistic respect for each other, there still existed a sort of armed neutrality which sometimes resulted in an outbreak of "rude letters" from me. He possessed a whole collection from my pen.

Thank goodness, he apparently took them as they were intended—as momentary outbursts of wrath not to be considered entirely seriously. In any case he told me later when I was leaving Hamburg that he had kept this unique collection for his own gratification, and would always read the letters when he was in a bad temper.

"So now I know," was my final dig, "that you'll often think of me. . . ."

My new agent, Salter, was very active in my interests; he sent me a contract for two performances of Sophie in *Rosenkavalier* under Beecham at Drury Lane in London. Frieda Hempel was the Marschallin and Bohnen, Ochs von Lerchenau; in conjunction with this, Agathe and Eva at the Cologne Festival. Then in August, after a short holiday, Agathe at the Zoppoter Waldoper. Everywhere he had insisted on a fee beyond my wildest dreams.

At the beginning of the year I sang at the magnificent celebrations of the silver wedding of Herr Ballin, the man-

123

aging chairman of the Hamburg-American line, and at this wonderful festival I met one of the directors, John Naht and his wife, who immediately offered spontaneously to accompany me to London, when I confessed I was a little frightened at my first venture into a strange country. We became great friends during a lovely week-end stay at Hamfeld, the Ballin's feudal estate near Hamburg, and sure enough, on the first day of July we set off for London.

It was then 1914. . . .

London made a tremendous impression on me. Its immense, seething life, the magnificent parks with their marvelous stretches of lawn and no police regulations about walking on them, the incredible display of flowers—I spent a rushed three days among them and sang twice with pleasing success.

"Covent Garden next time," said John Naht, pointing out the plain old box of a building in the middle of London's fruit market which scarcely suggests that behind its ugly gray walls the world's loveliest voices foregather every year.

My new friends took me as far as Cologne. And here too I met my dear mother, whom I wanted to send to Neuenahr where a thorough cure might help her poor stomach. Father had gone to Hiddensee from which he wouldn't be parted.

Freischütz was effectively produced and conducted by Hans Pfitzner and *Tannhäuser* by Gustav Brecher, whom I greeted again with delight, proud at having made such progress in the interim. Pfitzner, after my departure, wrote to say that he saw in me one of the greatest hopes of the German stage. He only hoped that I would never become a "rehearsal-shy"

124

prima donna but would always remain just as industrious, and always bear in mind that one never "gets there."

In Neuenahr I met my mother looking better than I had ever seen her. The peaceful, carefree life and the excellent treatment had worked wonders. Life had now become a magic tablecloth for us with my fine fees as the swiftly learned magic formula. . . . Wonderful walks through the Ahr Valley and an unforgettable trip down the Rhine—all those we enjoyed with the wonderment of children round the Christmas tree.

Then came Zoppot and the *Freischütz* performances in the middle of the German pine forest with Richard Tauber as Max.

I have hardly ever seen the *Freischütz* so enchantingly produced as it was there by the greatest of all producers— Nature. Again and again we were thrilled by the enchanting poetry of our forest setting. Only once I cursed the darkness of the pines when with the cry of joy, "Sweetly enraptured, to him!" I had to rush into my Max's arms. I had won a forfeit from Tauber, and the uncommonly tempting reward was to be a bar of chocolate.

"Where is my chocolate, Richard?" were my first words that evening as I took my place behind the two screens made of interwoven pine branches which hid us from the audience.

"You'll get it when you least expect it." Max prophesied with a mischievous smile.

"As long as it doesn't make us laugh!" whispered Ännchen to me in a worried tone.

125

The music started, the green screens were pushed aside; before us was the audience of several thousand people; above us, in the light of the powerful lamps, countless night-moths gleamed silver. Weber's true German music—and around us the dark German forest. . . .

"Sweetly enraptured, to him!" I exulted and ran into the dark pines where my Max awaited his entry.

He pressed something into my hand, murmured, *"j'y pense,"* and dragged me on to the scene, into the blinding glare of the floodlights.

Now wasn't it thoughtful of him? Max had brought a bar of chocolate for his Agathe, all wrapped up in silver paper. . . . But Agathe's fear for her Max seemed even greater than her joy: I quickly laid the marvelous present on a bench where it gleamed treacherously in the full illumination. Ännchen with great presence of mind sat on it and couldn't be moved from her place all the rest of the act. It was a terribly funny situation. So as to avoid catching each other's eye—for then what would have become of our hardly maintained self-control—we spoke and sang past each other. And it is the absolute truth that later an acquaintance of mine in the audience told me that he had thought that we were particularly moved and had really caught the proper atmosphere in that very scene. He had had the impression that I could scarcely speak for tears.

And I didn't betray to him the fact that they were tears of laughter!

126

CHAPTER
ELEVEN

INTO the middle of those lovely carefree days, the hand of a wrathful God threw his ghastliest thunderbolt. War threatened annihilation to the world.

We left Zoppot in terror and hurried home to the dark uncertainty of the future, alarmed by the wildest rumors. While we waited for hours in the railway station, which was thrown into sudden confusion, we saw the first troop trains bearing their load of young, high-spirited men, confident of victory, off to the front, singing amidst the cheers.

"War!" pealed the bells from the towers, bells that had been cast as voices of peace.

In fearful uncertainty we forgathered in the theater. Would we go on playing, would people still want to go to the theater while so many, so incalculably many were dying outside?

But everything went on. People needed more than ever to be distracted and elevated—and to forget. We artists also took part in the general effort to do something for this "great time," and we wore ourselves out at countless charitable institutions and hospital performances. One feature which happened regularly once a week the entire duration of the war, in which we all took part countless times, was the military matinees, energetically run and financed by Frau Tony Seligmann in aid of the children's soup kitchen, and to entertain the wounded soldiers who were constantly appearing in large numbers. It was a strenuous time—in the afternoons I would frequently sing once or twice in hospitals even when I had something on at night. We all wanted to do our bit.

In November came my guest season in Vienna.

The gay brilliance of the old Imperial city, as I drove through it with a beating heart, made me quite forget that the black shadows of this terrible war threatened it too. The whole life and bustle seemed so carefree, so full of joy and the love of gaiety. I entered that magnificent, imposing building, the Court Opera House, with a feeling of awe. I was singing Eva and had a rehearsal with Franz Schalk. Richard Mayr, Weidemann, Miller and the others were already assembled in the rehearsal room. Schalk made me think of some incredibly fine courtier as he came up to greet me with his nervous strutting gait. I thought I could read something suspiciously like mockery in the depths of the courteous distrait glance he gave me. I wasn't acquainted with him, so I didn't know that he liked nothing new. Everyone who came from outside was for him first and foremost just "provincial." And no one who had not been impregnated with the sacred traditions of the Vienna Court Opera was for him really worthy to sing or even to call him-

128

self an artist. . . . But who was so highly qualified to preserve the priceless heritage of this tradition—who served as selflessly as he the work and the institution he loved with every heartbeat? He taught me, too, to love the Vienna Opera as an indestructible temple. I had his guidance as conductor and director, and my grateful respect for him remains unchanged.

As Eva I got a most friendly reception from the public and the press. Ludwig Karpath even wrote that there was every prospect of my speedily becoming a Viennese favorite. The performance, thrillingly conducted by Franz Schalk—I had never known such ecstatic abandon—the orchestra (the Philharmonic!)—everything made a tremendous impression on me. Hamburg suddenly seemed provincial—the opera I loved so well couldn't compare with this magnificent Court Opera in any respect. . . .

And how nice they all were to me: Von Wymetal, the chief producer, took me himself to the wardrobe room so that I could see the lovely costumes Alfred Roller had designed for Eva; in case I didn't like them, others would be laid out for my inspection! That sort of thing didn't happen in Hamburg.

Of course this appealed to me enormously!

Only one thing made me feel quite strange: a man came to my door at the hotel and addressed me urgently and mysteriously through the dividing wall. At first I didn't know what he wanted until at last I heard the word "claque."

129

I burst out laughing. So they did have that here, as my Hamburg colleagues had predicted.

"No, no, I don't want a claque," I cried to him, "I won't pay for my applause. It's a frightful idea. . . ."

"Think of your career," came the urgent whisper behind the door. But I remained deaf to his entreaties and at last his ghostly tread took a hesitating departure.

An hour later, smuggled in in some cunning way, a man with a smug, foxy face stood before me, with orders and medals hanging curiously on his coat.

"I've come about the claque this evening," he said clicking his heels and bowing deeply.

"But, I've already told you I don't want it," I answered impatiently.

"Oh, that was Wessely. I haven't been here—so Wessely's been here. . . ."

He shook his fists accusingly to Heaven at this infamous rival. No, he was the real "Chief of Staff Officer" of the claque, esteemed by all. Indeed it seemed to me from what he told me that he must be the chief person in the Opera House. . . . Under his arm he carried a packet of old newspapers, in every pocket gilt postcards and letters with contracts for applause which had been sent to him in strictest confidence, and which he only wanted to show me as a proof of his eminence. At last I had to acknowledge it—one must have him. . . .

When, on the evening, among the enthusiastic calls for

Weidemann, Miller, Mayr and Heydter, a few "Lehmanns" were mingled, I wished I could fall through some friendly trap door; "Freudenberger's doing his bit . . ." I thought with shame, and scarcely enjoyed my success at all.

But what did my success matter in that performance! I felt quite dazed. The most wonderful orchestra in the world had borne my voice on harmonies of incredible sweetness into a house of resplendent and festive grandeur. I still see Weidemann's Sachs in all its dignity and simple poetry, and Mayr's Pogner! Who can strike the dark-vibrating note of deepest humanity with such blessed loveliness as he with his rich warm bass? I went home to my hotel, having listened rather than sung. . . .

CHAPTER
TWELVE

WHEN I returned to Hamburg and penitently greeted the beloved town with its amosphere of home, I suddenly felt uprooted. The fascinating foreign atmosphere of Vienna—would it ever become the atmosphere of home for me? I was Nordic—very German. The light quick blood of the Austrians did not flow in my veins. Would my heart ever beat to the same rhythm?

I still felt a fervent adherence to Hamburg—for the time being, at least.

Penitently, as though I had committed a severe breach of faith, I returned to my old home, and should have liked to greet the slightly despised opera house that looked so gray and bare and unfestive, with jubilant song, out of sheer joy at seeing it again. Now that I knew that I must leave it—for my Vienna contract was now confirmed—I was twice as fond of it and everything that meant Hamburg.

And the audience seemed to feel the same way.

I now had confirmation from the great exacting world outside that I deserved my success. So now everyone was rather proud of me and would have liked to say "she belongs

to us." And now I wanted to go. . . . In spite of all the privations of war, this last time in Hamburg was the best of all. I
was loaded with love and admiration, the flowers never
withered in my vases, my "stage-door admirers" grew to
considerable numbers. During this last period we lived on
the Holzdamm, right on the Alster, opposite the big convent-
school. The flappers joined headlong in the Lehmann-craze
and were often a real nuisance. . . . They always knew when I
had a rehearsal, and waited in troops before my front door
whenever they possibly could. At first they were content to
greet me radiantly and then rush away ecstatically. But gradually they became cheekier. They simply lay in wait for me,
and Lotte the housemaid had the greatest difficulty in ward-
ing them off when they came "to say something very important" to me, or at least to see me just for a moment, "just
for a moment!" they pleaded. But Lotte stood before the
door, her arms stretched out dramatically. She was very
young and imaginative and, really only half a child like the
others, was carried away on this whirl of adoration. On the
many occasions when she was allowed to go to the opera,
she would act like a madwoman the whole day. She particularly liked operas where I wore a crown. This seemed to
her the only style worthy of me. . . . My young friends used to
tell me that in the gallery she had whole crowds round her to
whom she would proudly say: "You can see her now, but I
see her every day. I see her in bed and simply everywhere.
For she is my mistress."

Then she would lie herself black in the face about how I always went around in trailing regal robes—and all sorts of other nonsense.

She was bitterly disappointed that I was quite different in reality. When she saw me as Recha in the *Jüdin,* she was deeply mortified at the rags I had to perish in. But when the executioners threw me into the pot, she bellowed in despair: "They're throwing my mistress into the boiling oil. . . ."

At my car door at the stage entrance she carried on worst of all, and climbed up beside the chauffeur like a conquering hero. It was only with difficulty that I could dissuade her from singing to Dr. Loewenfeld. She could do Elsa "quite perfectly" and believed she would be engaged on the spot. Her devastating singing had constantly to be "choked off.". . . But the enmity between her and the flappers became so great that she brusquely threw out her rivals as soon as they asked for me. One day I got a letter from Eddi who has since become a dear friend of mine suggesting that when I was at home and wanted to see them I should hang a little flag out of my window. . . . But even though I laughingly declined the little flag they used to sneak in to me and bring their homework, which I corrected with pleasure when I found time, rejoicing over a good mark and indignant when "our" exercise wasn't considered good. . . .

For many months a modest little bunch of lilies of the valley lay on my dressing table, always the same flowers whatever the season. A little note was attached with "Mia" on it. Nothing else. Often, when I was leaving by car a hand would furtively press lilies of the valley into mine and vanish without a trace. I wanted to get glimpse of this Mia who so persistently loved and eluded me. So one evening I kept a sharp lookout—and caught a violently struggling girl's hand.

"Mia," I said, and looked laughingly into a pair of lovely blue eyes, "I simply must know who you are! You've got to come and see me." So she came. No, no, she protested, she hadn't wanted to make my acquaintance. She wanted to keep her dream to herself. . . . She looked at me almost mutinously. And that hour was the beginning of a great friendship. Mia now lives in Atlanta, Georgia. But we see each other every year. She comes to me and brings her pale, lovely, black-haired child to see its godmother—little Mialotte. And I have often driven through endless cotton fields to visit her in her wonderful white house.

Toward the end of my last season came the first performance of D'Albert's *Tote Augen*—I was the first to sing Myrtocle and my great success set the final seal, so to speak, on my Hamburg career. Bürs was a moving Arcesius; Maclenan, Captain Galba; and Drill-Orridge, a serenely beautiful Mary Magdalene. Dr. Loewenfeld really let himself go in a riot of exotic coloring, his unappeasable thirst for color could scarcely be satisfied. How long did he not take before he finally painstakingly selected the right tone for the carpet on which I had to walk in the shimmering orange-colored robes of the blind Greek girl! This is the scene where

135

her sight is restored: Myrtocle, blind no longer, stumbles on to the stage, and her first cry in a world newly revealed to her is: "A mirror!" . . . I refused to sing that. D'Albert tried in vain to explain to me that psychologically it was quit correct, that the blind woman should want to see her own face before anything else.

"Then I can't sing the part," I declared categorically. "I don't feel it like that, so I can't play the scene as I imagine it."

Dr. Loewenfeld nodded soothingly at D'Albert: "You let Lehmann do it. She's sure to be good."

And at the stage rehearsal D'Albert was quite delighted with this very scene.

It was a great popular success. The unpretentious melody "Amor and Psyche" in the first act nearly became a "hit." I had to sing it at every concert—even later, when I came back as a guest—and the loud demand that rose, particularly from my faithful flappers, for "Amor and Psyche" made it a permanent item on my repertoire of encores.

The newspapers continued to say that I should have remained in Hamburg, and now Dr. Loewenfeld was willing to pay me any fee if I would only give up Vienna and decide to stay in Hamburg. I loved Hamburg and felt that I belonged there. Many a letter was dispatched to the Vienna director with the request that I might be released from my contract. Many a bitter tear I wept over his invariable and inexorable "No!"

It didn't occur to me that it would have been the greatest

136

blunder I could have made to exchange Hamburg for Vienna, and that I should be profoundly and eternally thankful for that "no!" Artistically and spiritually I found my home in Vienna—a home more lovely and satisfying than I could ever have dreamed.

I was to make my farewell appearance in *Tote Augen*. My heart was heavy, oh so heavy, as for the last time I climbed the steep old stairs to the dressing rooms. My tears fell as soon as I opened the door and saw how beautifully my dressing room had been decorated by good old Hulda Wolf, once so strict, and my dear Else. There were flowers everywhere: round the mirror, the chair, the table and the door. . . .

"Oh you're making it so difficult for me," I cried in tears. "How I wish I could stay here with you! But what can I do, I must go."

The audience covered me with tokens of love, and a regular shower of flowers fell on me. I could scarcely sing for emotion. I thanked them with my whole heart in trembling words which could hardly express my feelings, and when the storm of applause had subsided I trotted back to my dressing room like a sick person.

Then two days later came my farewell concert, and I felt with deep happiness that it was really true what Heinrich Chevalley wrote in the *Fremdenblatt*, that they loved me so much that it was like letting a beloved child go from the parental home: they were full of pride to see me go out into the great world, but also very anxious that everything should go

137

well with me. And I would be accompanied by the truly sincere wishes of all who knew and admired and loved me.. . .

Late into the night a particularly persistent group stood in front of my home, singing and shouting: "Hurrah for Lehmann," *"Au revoir!"* and "Come again!" Half dead from being feted I went out again on the balcony with only a coat thrown over me and shouted down vows of fidelity through the warm June night to the tarrying enthusiasts. Finally I said in despair: "Children, I beg you—go home now! 'Hurrah for Lehmann' is too noisy for a lullaby. And I'd really like to go to sleep. . . ."

The train that bore me off on my golden holidays sang its dear old childhood's song: "I think I can, I think I can."

"I think I can . . ." was the message of my heart to Vienna, which lay before me like a shining citadel I must conquer. Little did I dream—when I set out to conquer—that I should so soon capitulate to her beauty, her overwhelming charm and her captivating amiability. And that Hamburg would fade like a far, friendly picture that one keeps as a pleasant memory—but without longing. For in Vienna I found every fulfillment.

138

CHAPTER
THIRTEEN

I CAME to Vienna at a difficult time: the privations of the war weighed like a dark cloud on the formerly gay city— two years of war had considerably altered the picture which I had retained from my guest season. The streets were dirty and neglected—dust and paper whirled through the air when the wind swept the narrow streets, and my eye, accustomed to strict German orderliness, regarded with disapproval what I readily condemned as "slovenliness.". . . But the wide corridors that led to the door of the Opera director, the stately black-clad servitors who guarded the entrance, the solemn ceremony of being announced I found almost bureaucratic. . . .

The director, Herr Gregor, laughingly bade me welcome. "So I've really caught you," he said pleasantly—and his unmistakable German accent was music in my ears. . . . What made me so attached to Hamburg, he wanted to know. Wasn't I glad to be in Vienna? "Good Heavens—Vienna! You surely must feel it . . . it's a very special atmosphere. You watch: you'll fall hopelessly in love with Vienna. It's

139

just like getting into a bath that's got a bit too hot. First it's unpleasant and you want to get out. Then it begins to feel comfortable and gradually you get a bit hazy and dreamy, you feel lazy and sleepy and think it's very nice . . . and then you've already become Viennese yourself. . . ."

Thoroughly confused, I left Herr Gregor.

At my debut I sang Agathe in the *Freischütz*. The costumes I found fabulously beautiful, and was very surprised when I was urged to have new clothes made at the theater costumier's if I had any particular desires. I was amazingly lacking in vanity and scarcely looked in the mirror even to see whether anything fitted me and suited my face, and Wymetal, the chief producer, smilingly prophesied that I would soon be shedding that nonchalance and take more interest in my costumes; the refined Viennese taste would soon have an educative effect on me. I found Wymetal an irresistible charmer. His courtly distinguished manner and his amiable wit won all hearts. He chaffed me a good deal about my impulsiveness, a characteristic I shall unfortunately never get rid of, and scolded me a lot with an amused smile still in his eyes. It was some time before he really trusted me: behind my only too straightforward frankness he probably at first suspected the intention of making myself conspicuous. Nothing was more foreign to my nature. Only it was hard for me to cross the smoother parquet of the Court Opera after the good old Hamburg stage where I knew every worker and was good friends with all and sundry—"our

Lotte" to young and old. . . . In Vienna, in spite of fine successes I was naturally overshadowed by great names and personalities. Schalk, later—very much later—my best friend at the Opera, whom I love and revere beyond the grave, treated me more like a talented beginner, found fault a great deal—and I quickly learned the meaning of the Viennese word *sekkant**. Always ready with a quick unconsidered word, I found him difficult of approach. My colleagues were nice, but I longed to be in Hamburg, back in the circle of the friends who had surrounded me on the stage—for Vienna was very strange to me and seemed unwilling ever to reveal itself as my home. I shall never forget how warmhearted and good Bella Paalen was to me from the very first, and I am forever bound to her in sincere friendship.

It was a time when a number of artists of the highest quality flourished at the Opera. Maria Jeritza, Selma Kurz, Lucie Weidt, Marie Gutheil-Schoder, Berta Kiurina, Elisa Elizza, Bella Paalen, Hermine Kittel—I am grateful to them all for the great impression they made on me. Richard Mayr, Friedrich Weidemann, Leo Slezak, Erik Schmedes, Alfred Piccaver, Georg Maikl—what times those were! How often, listening up in the artists' box, I forgot stupid little personal grievances and even my homesickness for Hamburg. . . . They already wanted me back as a guest, but I couldn't be spared. I sang a great deal—and when Richard Strauss's *Ariadne*

---

* The nearest English equivalent is "teasing," but with a biting, sardonic undertone.

came out in autumn—actually the first appearance of the new version—I was given the rôle of the young composer in the prelude. But—only in the second cast. . . . While I studied I felt how marvelously it suited me. But I so much admired Gutheil-Schoder who was going to do the *première*, that I scarcely felt any bitterness at being "number two" with perhaps little prospect of getting to sing it for some time. I had seen Gutheil's overwhelming Elektra and her Octavian—and was quite under the spell of her highly spiritual art.

During the final rehearsals Gutheil was indisposed with a cold and I was called upon to take her place, and pleased Strauss so much that he gave me the *première* to do, as Gutheil had not recovered. There was, of course, a certain risk—perhaps he did hesitate and want to postpone the performance. . . . I don't know. In any case I was suddenly plunged headlong into the sensation of a Strauss *première* with Jeritza as Ariadne and Kurz as Zerbinetta. . . . From the friendly semi-obscurity of decent repertoire success I was suddenly pushed into the glaring limelight, and I read in a leading paper the next morning: "Last night at half-past eight, the whole of Vienna, so to speak, knew the name of Lehmann."

CHAPTER
FOURTEEN

AS IN a kaleidoscope these pictures pass through my mind: intensive work with Wymetal who taught me the beauty of gestures; singing Sieglinde with Schmedes; Octavian with Richard Mayr, the incomparable, the unforgettable; my first Manon with Piccaver, whose velvety voice was and is my great love; the enchanting sweetness of Kurz; the elemental Tosca of Jeritza; Gutheil, always my admiration and model; Paalen's magnificent Fides; Slezak's Otello and his terrific Eleazer. . . . Aagard Oestvig, who came like a meteor, blinding and sparkling—young, handsome, genial— a dreamlike Lohengrin. It is like a vivid picture book of song. . . .

Personally I still didn't feel quite at home; I was quickly pushed to the front, and one uncrowned queen of the Opera didn't like that. . . . For the first time in my life, I believe, I encountered veiled hostility. I learned that the way upward can also be an ugly and obnoxious competitive struggle, a struggle in which spiritually I must always be worsted, for when I am forced to fight I fight with open visor. . . . In my heart I have never had much sympathy with the idea of the

143

prima donna assoluta. . . . There is room for so many. . . .
The stronger the personality of the artist, the less meaning the
term "competition" has for him. Can't one love Rembrandt
and also be fascinated by Cézanne? Didn't I love the ele-
mentally sensual Salome of Jeritza just as much as the per-
versely lustful one of Guthiel—"Princess of Judæa" in every
inch? . . . One should get new corroboration and consolida-
tion of one's own personality from others. . . . There is something undignified about this petty fighting for oneself.

In general, artists are a great army fighting under one
flag; ready to help one another, understanding, good comrades. One must just forget a few unfortunate experiences. . . .

The Emperor Franz Joseph I died. The Opera was closed
for mourning and at once there was a telegram from Hamburg. "How many guest performances can you come for?"
I rushed to Lion, the secretary of the theater and later the
assistant director. Lion was what is known as "indispensable." He had an inimitable way of dealing with all the
tempers, hysteria and madnesses that went on round him,
with smiling superiority. So for days he found the right words
to soothe me, too, while I had to sit idly in Vienna when I
longed to be off to Hamburg. . . . I couldn't get permission to
give any guest performances. Nobody knew for certain when
Emperor Carl would open the Opera House again. And
while we were waiting, the longed-for opportunity for a guest
performance was slipping by. . . . Finally I lost my patience
and raged away to Lion over the fussy formalities there. . . .

144

Lion suddenly became very serious. He seized the telephone and asked to be put through to Fürst Montenuovo.

Then I got thoroughly frightened.

"Herr Lion, I didn't really mean it . . . you're not going to report me, are you?"

"That was *lèse-majesté*," he said, as solemn as a judge, and related word for word through the telephone what I had said. . . .

In those moments of fear I simply couldn't imagine what the consequences of my thoughtless words might be. I didn't see that with his other hand Lion was pressing down the receiver so that the line was "dead," and it was only when he said: "What was that, Your Excellency? I'm to send for a mental doctor and have Fräulein Lehmann taken away in a straight jacket?" that I noticed that it had all been a joke, and breathed again. . . . Later, among his friends, Lion often described this scene—and many others—where my impulsiveness and lack of self-discipline brought me into similar situations. From this hour he was my special friend and when he left us a year later, I regretted it with all my heart.

After this involuntary vacation I had a great deal to sing. I came to the rescue of sick colleagues, and what with rehearsals and performances, I was scarcely off the stage.

Vienna began to feel more like home. . . . There were still guest performances in Hamburg and tearful farewells when I had to leave, but Vienna . . . the magic of that wonderful city began to work on me and hold me fast. . . . Yes,

145

even those "court-ceremonies" made a great impression on me, when at a gala concert in the great hall of the Konzerthaus, the young Imperial pair made their first official appearance. I sang along with Jeritza, Kurz, Weidt and Slezak, Mayr and Piccaver. Nor did the fact that I heard a few sneering remarks about my dress spoil the great impression of that festive occasion. For it simply hadn't occurred to me that this was an evening to which one must come "in all one's grandeur"—clothes just didn't interest me and I wore some old thing that had originated in Hamburg—so I probably did look like Cinderella among my colleagues. But it was a lesson to me. Never again would I stand among the others looking like an interloper. . . . So I went the very next day to a great salon and ordered something expensive and good. . . .

In my second year I was engaged by the Red Crescent to give some recitals in Constantinople.

The gorgeous Orient . . . veiled women seated motionless on the banks as I walked along the Golden Horn with speedily found friends. They looked after the motorboat unmoved, dumb to our merry salutations. . . . A visit to the old seraglio . . . Turkish coffee in tiny golden bowls set with brilliants . . . a rose from the harem garden . . . the Hagia Sophia! Ancient Ottomans kneeling on prayer mats—silently stepping on sacred ground . . . the bazaar, like a picture from the *Arabian Nights* . . . the beggars' quarter in Stamboul . . . the Island of Princes . . . feasts, receptions . . . the journey home through Bulgaria and Serbia. . . .

146

Then Vienna—poor, starving Vienna in the last year of the war. . . . Then at last, at long last, peace! We entered into this peace through the door of revolution. But all politics are discordant. . . . We artists live in a world of our own— beyond all politics. That is our vocation—to serve a Divinity that unites the nations and knows nothing of strife and dissension.

Two dear friends from Hamburg came to Vienna—Elisabeth Schumann and Friedrich Weidemann. They were a great success and soon felt at home in "my" town, for so Vienna had become. I loved it, I still love it! It is my refuge and my home.

At the *première* of *Sister Angelica*, I made the acquaintance of that wonderful composer, Puccini. He came to Vienna with his friend and accompanist, Riccardo Schnabl-Rossi and attended one rehearsal, where his sensitive Italian ear was not quite satisfied with some of the voices. In a bad humor he said to Riccardo: "Do go to the rehearsal of *Suor Angelica:* I'd like to know what ignoramus is singing Angelica. . . ."

Riccardo has often told me how he listened to me for a few minutes and than ran back to Puccini crying: "You'll be delighted. . . ."

"Oh, you're exaggerating. . . . You've always had this weakness for Vienna. . . ."

But I really think Puccini was satisfied with me. I have a photograph of him with the dedication: "To the incomparable

147

Angelica." And when he saw me as Mimi, his tears told me more than any words. . . .

The revolution was infectious: a bad crisis broke out in our Opera House too. Gregor resigned—and in his place came the double directorate of Strauss-Schalk. Richard Strauss lent the Opera House the luster of his great name, and gave some wonderful evenings. But Franz Schalk devoted his life and soul and entire strength. . . . One could have safely predicted that the joint rule of two such dissimilar natures couldn't last. It soon led to great misunderstandings between the two, and this did not do the Opera any good.

One high point occurred during this directorate—the first performance of Strauss's *Frau ohne Schatten.* There was a magnificent cast with Jeritza as the Kaiserin, Weidt as the Nurse, Mayr as Barak and Oestvig as the Kaiser. I was the Dyer's Wife and found her an enthralling task. Schalk had sent the part to me at my holiday retreat at Gmunden on the Traunsee. I tried to study it by myself, but was glad when Leo Sirota, the pianist, took pity on me and sacrificed many hours of his holiday to coaching me in the extraordinarily difficult part of which Strauss himself had said jokingly to me that he scarcely believed it would be learned.

One very nice thing happened during this semi-holiday: I sang at a charity concert (in aid of a home for consumptives), and the Duke of Cumberland was present with his entire family. I was invited to their lovely old castle and spent a charming evening in the domestic circle of the ducal

An Early Picture as the Young Composer in *Ariadne auf Naxos,*
My First Important Success.

house. Naturally I sang a few songs, and the Duchess of Brunswick, the daughter of the German Kaiser, afterward sent me her photograph and a charming pearl brooch. The old Duke laughed a great deal over my theater anecdotes and I was asked back again. What would I have said in earlier years if someone had prophesied that one day I would be chatting away with Kaiser Wilhelm's daughter? . . . In those days in Berlin I used to wait hours on Sundays Unter den Linden to see the "little Princess" go past and wave to her. . . .

Richard Strauss summoned me to Garmisch. He wanted to give me a detailed coaching in the important rôle of the Dyer's Wife, before the ensemble-rehearsals started at the beginning of the season. I spent very happy hours at Garmisch studying with him. There, at the piano, he was lord and master. . . .

CHAPTER
FIFTEEN

IN THE spring of 1922 I went to South America under the management of Mocchi, the famous Italian impresario. The good old Italian ship, *Tomaso di Savoia,* was almost entirely occupied by artists: the Italian company under Mascagni with Gilda dalla Rizza, Stabile and other illustrious names, and ours under Weingartner: with Helene Wildbrunn and her husband, our producer, Walter Kirchhoff, Emil Schipper and Carl Braun. Mascagni would have nothing to do with us Germans. Perhaps it was a feeling of enmity left from the war, perhaps he feared our rivalry. . . . In any case he gave us a wide berth during the three weeks of the voyage; our Italian colleagues, on the other hand, were all very nice to us. I was particularly friendly with Helene Wildbrunn. She is a wonderful artist, warmhearted and inspired—and she is a truly fine and kindly person. What a pity she retired so early from the stage—and how good that she imparts her rich experience to a circle of students who can be sure of her devotion to any task she undertakes!

The voyage was wonderful: phosphorescent fishes in a

shimmering deep-green sea, like stars fallen from some flashing southern evening sky . . . the drowsy heat of the equator . . . flying fish with silver sparkling fin-wings . . . the Southern Cross rising in the sky as the Great Bear set . . . the Brazilian coast . . . Santos . . . noisy Buenos Aires . . . the wonderful villa-quarter of Palermo with its incredible palaces, rows of jewelers in the principal street, with brilliants, pearls and emeralds worthy of a maharajah in their windows. . . .

It was the first time that Wagner had been sung by a German company. We all had an enormous success—we became a sensation, and our German performances were sold out.

And yet I was so little accustomed to being away from my family—separated from all I loved, by a boundless ocean— that I suffered terribly from homesickness and didn't really enjoy our time at Buenos Aires. My parents, during my absence, had gone to my brother who, now happily married, was spending the summer months with his wife and parents in his enchanting old Friesian house in Westerland, on the North Sea island of Sylt. So I knew that my parents were in good hands. But I longed for them, and would gladly have exchanged South America for quiet holiday weeks on the shores of the North Sea. At that time I hadn't that passion for traveling in my blood that later made me so restless, and still drives me through the world today. . . .

When the Vienna Philharmonic Orchestra came to Buenos

Aires and gave triumphant concerts under Weingartner, I
sat in the hall in floods of tears, listening with emotion to
the true German music of the *Meistersinger* Prelude, with
which the first concert opened—it brought back my native
land to me with overpowering effect in that foreign country.
All the dear familiar faces up on the platform, the luscious
sound of a Viennese orchestra—it was almost too much for
me. . . . I should have liked best to sail straight back home.
But my contract still took me to Montevideo for one performance of *Valkyrie* and to Bahia Blanca for a lieder-recital.
At that time I still gave very few concerts. The door to that
holy of holies, the "lied," had not yet opened to me. . . . I
had still no proper approach to it, and it was only later,
after years of experience with Ferdinand Foll and Leo Rosenek, that I gained my knowledge and mastery of its style.

My success at Bahia Blanca was of course in no way dimin-
ished by the fact that I didn't understand a great deal about
the lied. It was the very first time that any German lieder-
singer had ever come to that district, and members of the
German colony told me that they thought of a singer more as
a castanet-snapping Spanish woman, and didn't understand
it at all when a lady in a simple evening dress sang simple
songs in a foreign language without any gestures or "fuss.". . .
At the beginning of the recital the audience scarcely applauded at all, but gradually the magic of the song conquered there too, and I had even to repeat the concert a few
days later. The German colony gave a garden party in my

152

honor where a "native touch" was introduced in the form of an ox roasted while on the spit by an old Indian. And I—poor wretch—although all that flesh crackling on the open fire made me feel quite sick, had to choke down dreadful smoky chunks with smiles and words of praise. . . .

I went home on the little German steamer *Galicia,* and after many adversities in a violent storm in the Gulf of Santa Catarina, we arrived very late at Hamburg, having been over four weeks at sea. . . . At Teneriffe, the first port of call—so longed for after those eighteen days on the sea—I was given a present of two sweet tiny little dogs, "genuine Maltese"—who forthwith grew to be huge fellows of undefinable but amazingly mixed breed. Teneriffe lay like a fairy island in the golden light of the setting sun—the giant cliff all on fire with liquid gold. A proud sailing boat dipped its great white pinions in the blue and gold. . . . Boats swarmed round our ship with traders fluttering white tablecloths, artistic needlework, laces and scarves in the light, warm wind . . . animal-traders with "Teneriffe dogs" and bright-feathered birds . . . little boats laden with fruit all round us in wild confusion. . . .

My two dogs were restless cabin companions. I had christened them Max and Moritz—and they lived up to their names. . . .

Bilbao was the first European port to emerge after many days, and over us again shone the Great Bear—but the Southern Cross still rose like a distant dream over strange seas and shores. . . . When the first lights of Spain appeared,

153

there was great rejoicing in the steerage. Spanish emigrants were going home. . . . And they crowded to the side of the ship and greeted their regained land with songs and cries of jubilation. I often mixed with them and listened to their folk songs. That evening I saw a touching sight. An old Spaniard, bent and obviously very ill, crept up painfully to the others and sought for a place where he could see the lights, gaining it by soft entreaties. . . . And there he stood with both hands gripping the hard wood, the tears streaming down his wasting face, his sick old body shaken with unchecked sobs. Perhaps he was coming home to die on his sacred native earth. . . . It was the transfiguring radiance of his tired look that moved me so deeply. . . .

I had a joyful reunion with my people—but the new additions to the family, Max and Moritz, were not a success: they had a talent for transforming any room in a short time into a wild robbers' den, and their love of action too much exceeded their good will for them to be trained in habits of cleanliness. . . .

CHAPTER
SIXTEEN

AT LAST I was able to realize a lifelong dream—I bought my parents a house of their own at Hinterbrühl near Vienna. It took some time before they could move in, for we had it all newly done up but then it was a little gem. At that time I was in London, singing the Marschallin in *Rosenkavalier* under Bruno Walter at the opening performance of the Covent Garden season. I had sung Sophie as a young beginner, and later Octavian. But they needed a Marschallin for London, so I had accepted without betraying the fact that the part was quite new to me.

My first meeting with Bruno Walter—like that with Franz Schalk—gave no indication of the friendship and deep artistic understanding that later united us. I can imagine that he was not very pleased with me: the Marschallin is not a part that one can master at the first go. And Walter, with his passion for throwing light on every detail of a part, must have missed in me the entire exhausting of all the possibilities of the part. I confessed that I had never sung the Marschallin before and had only accepted for fear the lovely Covent Garden engagement would come to nothing—and I begged him to help me. Walter is happy when he can work. . . . I owe an endless amount to him during all the years that we have met again and again all over the world—at festivals, really festive under him!—London, Berlin, Paris, New York, Salzburg—in operas and concerts. How many old operatic parts became new and living under his direction! Often a word from him would make pale shadows flash into new life! My admiration for him is great and sincere. Colonel Eustace Blois was the manager of the Covent Garden Opera. Every inch an English gentleman, always pleasant, he was the most charming theater director I ever met! He was then hearing *Rosenkavalier* for the first time, and we almost envied him this great experience. What a cast: Richard Mayr as Ochs von Lerchenau. . . . That alone says a great deal.

Delia Reinhardt was enchanting as Octavian, Elisabeth Schumann the ideal Sophie . . . and Walter was at the conductor's desk. . . .

There were marvelous performances of the "Ring" with Lauritz Melchior, that triumphant heroic tenor, famed throughout the world as the greatest Wagner singer; Frieda Leider as a Brünhilde of grandiose harshness; Maria Olszewska, beautiful, interesting, temperamental; Friedrich Schorr, famous for his Wotan; Emil Schipper, a true German Hans Sachs; Maria Ivogün, an enchanting Zerbinetta—they all made an unforgettable impression on my life. Helene Wildbrunn's noble art, Sigrid Onegin's grandiose voice—I should

156

have to name them all individually if I were to do justice to the wonderful achievements of this company.

Walter soon called me to the Charlottenburg Opera where he was musical director for a few years. It was quite easy to captivate the enthusiastic warmhearted Berlin public. Guest performances at Charlottenburg and later at the State Opera soon made me very good friends with the appreciative Berliners. I look back on it all with emotion.

About this time I was invited by the Milan Scala to sing Eva in Italian under Toscanini. My refusal was one of the great blunders in life that can never be made good. I had always heard of the impatience, ruthlessness and self-will of the Mæstro, and it was simply fear of him that kept me from Milan. . . . So I foolishly threw away the artistic experience of making music with him. Years later, when my way finally crossed his, I learned to appreciate in full measure how much I had missed by that refusal.

In Autumn 1924 was the first performance of the musical comedy *Intermezzo* at Dresden. Strauss insisted on my singing Christine, a part which I refused at first, as I had the feeling that it did not suit me at all. In Christine he had glorified his beloved wife Pauline. The whole opera deals with an episode from his own life, he wrote the text himself, and the music, which frequently goes over into spoken tones, is novel and arresting. My friend Carl Alwin, conductor of the Vienna State Opera, a particularly enthusiastic Strauss admirer, coached me in the part and triumphantly

157

opposed all my repeated outbursts of violent refusal. . . . It is thanks to his tenacity that I did not give it up. Later I very much enjoyed this Christine; she was something new in my repertoire. Strauss heard me and was delighted that I so well understood his intention that the conversation set to music should be half-sung, half-spoken; he wrote to Fritz Busch at Dresden who was to conduct the first performance that everything I did was as he wished it. When we were saying good-by he told me that they weren't very pleased at having an outsider for the *première,* so I would just have to be "the great prima donna" with them. . . . But that wasn't my style at all. I was my natural self with everyone, made friends quickly, and greatly enjoyed the rehearsals with Fritz Busch and Mora, the producer—although they were all very astonished at my bold disregard of the notes. . . . Later Strauss did not permit this conversational nonchalance to my successor in the part. He wanted every note correctly sung— but with me he showed an almost childlike joy in Christine as I sang her.

My father said once to me when I got back to Vienna from Dresden that he would so much have liked to hear this very performance, and had been most disappointed that I hadn't taken him with me to Dresden.

"But Papa," I said laughingly, "nobody dreamed it would be a success. Schalk even said he was sorry I wouldn't be winning any laurels with that part which was so entirely opposed to my artistic nature. And just imagine if you'd seen

My Husband.

your daughter being a failure! That would have made you very unhappy, wouldn't it? The opera will soon come to Vienna and then you'll hear it. . . ."

But when *Intermezzo* was given in Vienna a few months later, my beloved father already lay out there in the churchyard. . . . Peacefully and unsuspectingly he had fallen asleep forever. He laughed a great deal that evening and played with his favorite Mohrle, the little black Pomeranian, and sang to himself as he went to bed. He probably went to sleep with the thought: "Tomorrow I'm going to Vienna to hear Lotte sing." But he never opened his eyes again. . . . It was a bolt from the blue. My mother became very ill, and for a long time we feared that she would never recover from the shock. Our doctor, Dr. Zifferer, stood by us, always a true friend and helper, and during all the years she survived my father, he cherished and tended my mother like a hothouse plant. Marie, her nurse, truest of the true, went through bad times before she slowly recovered. She remained devoted and true to her up to her last hours. I shall never forget that.

My dear father did not live to see my marriage, which would have made him very happy. After many obstacles and great struggles, I was able to unite myself officially to the man who has become my best and most understanding life's companion, Otto Krause. It is not easy to be the husband of an artist. It is a life that, with its constant ups and downs without rest or peace, its ambitions and torments of depression alternating with ecstatic joys, demands, even more than

an equable bourgeois disposition, a great deal of patient for-
bearance from one's life partner. . . . It indeed demands of
him a great deal of self-denial, consideration, understanding
and forgiveness. And the artist who can say: "This was and
is the right husband for me," has more reason to be grateful
to her fate than the majority of women. . . . I know it only
too well.

CHAPTER
SEVENTEEN

PUCCINI'S *Turandot* set me a new task. I must confess that this "Princess with the heart of ice" was not one of my favorite parts, and that I really enjoyed listening to Maria Nemeth's radiantly triumphant singing of Turandot more than singing it myself. . . . I studied this very difficult part with Felicia Kaszowska, who imparted to me a great deal of her rich fund of experience. She also helped me when I was studying *Fidelio* which, at Schalk's special request, I sang for the first time at the Beethoven Centenary. It was with great misgivings that I approached this part which really oversteps the limits of the lyric-dramatic and takes one into the realm of the dramatic. But I knew I could trust Schalk implicitly: he loved my voice and was intent on preserving and nursing it—he would not advise anything that could do it any harm.

Although my husband is not a practicing musician himself, he is deeply musical and full of understanding for my work and art. He is, moreover, my last "court of appeal." I am fortunate in having so beloved a counselor always at my side—and that objectivity which is one of his characteristics is unceasingly valuable to me. In the same way as he advises against a foolhardy attempt at high dramatic rôles which might injure my voice, he gives me also the necessary assurance to attempt a new part which I have perhaps stubbornly and foolishly resisted. He it was, for instance, who finally persuaded me to do a part which I had long resisted—Fidelio—and which became one of my best rôles.

Fidelio under Schalk was one of the greatest experiences in my life. The deep emotion with which he conducted this noble work, was apparent in every rehearsal. I often saw tears dim his eyes—and the fragile, elegant form at the piano, the nervous, slender, beautiful hands on the keyboard, and his spiritual face are all indelibly impressed on my memory. One had to know Schalk very well to realize what an extraordinarily fine man he was at heart. He hid his easily wounded soul behind mockery and malice. . . . His love of sharp repartee and his fear of showing himself as he really was, made him appear quite different from the man I believe I knew. I admired him very much and think back on him with loving gratitude.

Our *Fidelio* was a very great success.

After we had lost Wymetal to the New York Metropolitan Opera, Dr. Wallerstein, an artist of a new age, had come to our old Opera as producer. Incidentally it was he who first gave Schalk the idea of trying me as Fidelio—a suggestion for which I cannot be sufficiently grateful.

162

Everything new has its pros and cons . . . Wallerstein's sharp intellectual mind was perhaps too much focused on detail, and this had a dispersed effect and spoiled what should have made a more grandiose impression. But he soon adapted his ideas to the quieter sphere of Viennese taste, and the exaggerated mobility of his earlier performances achieved a greater repose. I have always liked working with him and got on very well with him, and I have seen productions of his of amazing unity and interest. In *Fidelio* he directed me very well. Schalk never bothered at all about the dramatic form of a new production. He was the faithful custodian of the music. He never interfered, not even by raising a single objection, at the rehearsals. But his mobile face revealed his pleasure and aversion like a mirror. . . .

Characteristic of the musical city of Vienna was the extent to which everything and everyone was affected by the Beethoven Centenary Festival. This festive event was the focal point of the entire life at this period. . . . Beethoven pictures, Beethoven music—the whole of Vienna was in unison. . . .

Fidelio was the climax—and we ourselves were borne to lofty heights on the ecstasies of an inspired rendering. . . .

Later we took this *Fidelio* to Paris and conquered the French with this most German of all German works. . . .

For the first time I saw Paris and fell an immediate victim to the irresistible charm that emanates from the gay life of that city. The brightly lit Champs-Elysées, the Palais de la

Concorde, the gay Bois de Boulogne—they have all for me
the essence of "beauty," like the emerald of England, the
cherry trees in blossom at Kew Gardens and the gorgeous
flower beds at Hampton Court. . . .

But can all those ever make me forget that darling holiday paradise so near to my heart, Hiddensee, the little island
on the Baltic? . . . The inhabitants affectionately call it *"dat
söte Länneken,"* which means "the sweet little land," and it
aptly describes the soft beauty of their home. How delightful
it is to look down from the edge of the wood to the waving
gold cornfields, over the flower-embroidered, gently down-
sloping meadows—over the narrow strip of land which in
one place separates the Baltic by only about a stone's throw
from the *Bodden,* the Shallows that resemble an inland
lake. Walking with bare feet along the meadow path with
the boggy floor caressing one's soles like cool velvet! Climb-
ing down through the romantic Swantiwitt ravine, overgrown with wild roses and still golden broom bushes, down
to the stony shore! Deep solitude! Only the murmur of the
waves and the cry of the gulls from the blue sky! We live in
a little wooden house, primitively like true forest folk. . . . A
big flag waves from our little roof, and on it stands in large
letters: *"Laat mi tofreden,"* "Leave me in peace." . . . We
have often heard Sunday trippers who have come over by
steamer from Stralsund spelling out the inscription . . . then
laughter . . . then silence . . . and frequently: "They're quite
right, the people in there. They want to be by themselves."

164

This is the only way to enjoy one's holidays. I often dream of how lovely it would be to live *always* under a flag like that: *"Laat mi tofreden. . . ."*

We spent many holiday weeks, too, in Sylt, at my brother's old Friesian house. He has made an exhaustive study of Friesian customs, and it is thanks to his influence that the old costumes have been revived. With endless trouble he has assembled a local museum, set up an open-air stage on the dunes with the most primitive means, and has written the most lovely open-air plays and performed them there with the local people. When the great causeway was opened connecting Sylt with the mainland, he organized a procession, a cavalcade of a hundred years, which necessitated a great knowledge of the folk life and history of the Friesians. The aged Hindenburg was a distinguished spectator at this procession. I particularly remember the final scene of one of those open-air plays of my brother's: the tall silhouette of a Friesian on the dunes against the evening sky, lit up by the flickering torch in his hand; the North Sea murmuring its eternal song as an accompaniment to the verse that came clearly through the July night to the many listeners.

The beauty of Sylt is harsh and wild. No tree can stand up to the severe Autumn storms. At only a few places in the shallows there are thick plantations of trees, and in a few sheltered parts too, behind strong high walls, trees and shrubs crouch near the sea. . . . But on the whole the island is bare and treeless. Gray heavy clouds frequently hang

165

threatening in the sky, storms race over the wide moors, hurl thundering mountainous waves on to the snowy white strand and inundate walls and piers. A storm on Sylt remains an unforgettable memory. . . . And on fine days, who can describe the joy of riding over the moors or along the shore at low tide! My husband, himself an excellent horseman, taught me this wonderful sport.

My husband practically grew up in the saddle. Born in Budapest, he came as a child to Vienna and was enrolled as a cadet in the school connected with the Artillery Corps. At fourteen years of age, he was already an accomplished young horseman. When he became an officer, he had further schooling in the official military cavalry division, took part in many official races, and won many prizes. I met him only after the downfall of the imperial government, when he had retired from the army, and so I never had the opportunity to see him as a cavalry rider. However, my opera colleague, Victor Madin, who as a young man had spent evening after evening next to my husband in the opera box reserved for army officers, once said to me in greatest amazement: "Gracious, you have never seen Otto ride? But that is grotesque. It is as strange as though he had never heard you sing."

Then I had an opportunity to see him in the famous Vienna "Spanish Riding School" riding one of the renowned snow-white Lippizaner stallions. He seemed as much a part of the magnificent horse as one of the noble centaurs of old. For the first time, I understood what the art of riding really meant.

166

In Westerland.

—*Foto Skall*, Wien

What a joy it was for me when he became also my riding instructor.

The loveliest hours of all my life were riding with him every morning through wind and weather over the brown, wind-tossed heather, or flying over the firm sand at full gallop beside the foaming sea. . . . Then back to one's beloved work, brown and strengthened, gloriously refreshed by the harsh, salty tang of the North Sea air!

The first call that summoned me to Paris, the heart of the "great world," had sounded in my life like a fanfare. . . . I was henceforth to count as an international celebrity. Suddenly there came a shower of requests for recitals from France, Belgium and Holland. . . . Guest performances at the Paris Grand Opera—and ever and again, Covent Garden in London. . . . Professor Ferdinand Foll, who had accompanied my first attempts at lieder-recitals in Vienna, gave me my first real idea of lieder-style. I still sang too robustly, not intimately enough. With all his benevolence and sensitive understanding, he was only once satisfied with me—when I sang Schumann's "Frauenliebe und -leben" with him in Vienna. Perhaps it was very near to his way of thinking, for while we were going from the platform of the Musikverein-saal back to the greenroom he said in his quiet way: "That was an experience for me. It was most beautiful. . . ."

This was the first praise he had ever bestowed on my lieder-singing and it made me shed proud and happy tears.

167

How often did he say to me: "You could be a quite great lieder-singer. But you must have patience and conquer this world for yourself, step by step; it is not a goal you can reach at the first onrush. . . ."

When Ferdinand Foll died, it was for me as if I had forever lost the possibility of becoming a lieder-singer.

Then I met Leo Rosenek. Only by intensive study and in the course of long concert tours over the whole of Europe did I enter this enchanted kingdom, whose conquest demands the highest artistic maturity.

And now when my revered friend Bruno Walter accompanies me on the piano at special recitals, and I enjoy the blissful sense of mutual understanding in our work together, I know that my studies with Rosenek helped to smooth the way for me.

Unfortunately I have never kept a diary nor made notes, so I shall perhaps be unable to give every incident in its proper order. But that is of no great importance. I write these reminiscences on my tours through America—and while express trains rush me through the deserts of New Mexico, through California orange groves and Canada's ice and snow, through the palm forests of Florida and the bare cheerless tracts of the Middle West, brightly colored butterflies flutter round me—changing pictures of memory. . . .

"Chamber-music singer to Austria." . . . Schalk, who, shortly after sharing the directorate with Strauss for two years, became sole director, caused this title, which had been abolished during the revolution, to be revived. I was the first "chamber-music singer" to be appointed by the new régime. Years later I was awarded the proud distinction of becoming an honorary member of the State Opera.

In 1928, during the most severe winter we had had for a long time, Schalk took our *Fidelio* company to Stockholm. That marvelous city, which we reached after fighting our way with difficulty over the frozen Baltic, lay deep in snow and ice. It was so bitterly cold that I hardly saw anything of Stockholm. After the performance we were received at Court, and the chief performers were awarded the Gold Medal for Art and Learning, which I proudly pinned on beside the Golden Palm which France had given me for *Fidelio*.

In London during the Covent Garden season we gave a charming performance of *Fledermaus* under Bruno Walter. We played in enchanting "Old-Vienna" costumes; Elisabeth Schumann was Adele, I was Rosalinde and Maria Olszewska was our Orlofsky. For the first time the English King and Queen attended a German performance, and during one of our intervals we were presented to Their Majesties.

The audience at Covent Garden is a brilliant spectacle, and we who, during the postwar years, had seen such really depressing sights in the stately Vienna Opera, took particular pleasure in the sight of the elegant English, the men in full evening dress or uniform, the women in magnificent gowns,

169

wearing priceless jewelry with perfect taste. Charming King Manuel of Portugal, who unfortunately died so early, and his lovable consort were great opera-enthusiasts. I made his acquaintance in an extraordinary way. I was giving a recital with Bruno Walter, and in the interval a very nice-looking young man, whose face was vaguely familiar to me, although I had no idea who he was, came into the greenroom. I went on looking through my music and paid no attention to him. With one ear I heard Walter calling him "Your Majesty," but I thought it must be a nickname, because this "Majesty" spoke with all the enthusiasm of a devotee addressing his idol. . . . He also paid me some charming compliments which I acknowledged with an absent-minded nod. It was only when he took his leave and I saw Walter's ceremonial bow and noticed the manager's deference that it began to dawn on me that I had again behaved in an unbecoming manner. . . .

"Who was that?" I asked in astonishment.

"That was King Manuel—and you treated him as if he had been a student from the top gallery. . . ."

Walter and I both laughed heartily. On later occasions I was often in the company of the Royal pair, who were very pleased when one talked quite unceremoniously. The King, who was very musical, was a warm admirer of Walter's. We went out to see Their Majesties at the beautiful castle where, amid masses of flowers, they had made their home. Once the King accompanied me on the organ and was as pleased as a boy about it.

170

It was sad to miss the two faces from the box they had occupied for years, when Manuel died unexpectedly, sincerely mourned by all who knew him.

I have many happy memories connected with London. The magnificent *Figaro* performance under Walter—the "Ring" with him and with Robert Heger—and again and again *Rosenkavalier,* which remained a standard item of the Covent Garden season. Dusty old stage decorations were the background to artistically incomparable performances. Covent Garden itself is an ugly building in the middle of London's fruit and vegetable market. . . . We had to climb up shaky old steps to rather doubtful dressing rooms—but we all felt at home there and scarcely noticed the grotesque incongruity between our frequently regally magnificent costumes and our surroundings. . . .

After Walter came Sir Thomas Beecham, and brought Dr. Erhardt with him as producer. Then came new ideas, modern productions, sparkling life, stage reconstructions—Sir Thomas, witty, elegant, with a genius for comedy. . . . Music danced in rainbow patterns through the stately house, an enthusiastic audience constantly filled balconies and boxes; now there was something to look at as well as to listen to!

Colonel Blois, our manager, was dead, Bruno Walter gone—*le roi est mort, vive le roi!*

CHAPTER
EIGHTEEN

IN 1927, I sang for the first time at the Salzburg Festival. In spite of all the festivities, Salzburg was still a quiet little town, wearing the festive garments of one summer month as bashfully as a young debutante her first ball-gown. There was still almost no indication of the enormous proportions that our Festival would gradually assume.

Our beautiful performance of *Fidelio* was constantly repeated, always with solemn joy. . . . There was *Rosenkavalier,* with Salzburg's great son, Richard Mayr, as the star . . . and heavenly Mozart. In the audience were music-lovers from all the countries of the world.

The first year I stayed the whole time at the Hotel am Forst in Bayrisch Gmain, that is, on the other side of the frontier. The inhaling cure did my voice good—and often, after a strenuous rehearsal, I used to sit in the little bathing cabin quite enveloped in the damp steam of the Reichenhall brine. Later, when the demands of the Festival constantly increased, I rented a villa quite near the town, like nearly all my colleagues.

172

I love swimming and can scarcely pass a swimming pool without yielding to temptation. Neither wind nor weather can stop me—and I once got a bad cold during the busiest festival-time, which, carelessly neglected, developed into proper influenza. Schalk visited me in Bayrisch Gmain—and when he heard how my illness had originated he said with a shake of his head: "What does a singer want with cold water? If I could only interfere in your private life I should engage a keeper for you; the way you treat your valuable throat is really too dangerously reckless!"

But I have found that it is much better to harden yourself than to go about with a handkerchief held protectively before your mouth, as so many singers do. Familiarity with water, wind and rain is the best protection against colds.

But from wind and rain my thoughts fly to the Riviera. . . . I go there almost every year, have sung in Nice, Monte Carlo and Cannes, and have always enjoyed a few free days' holiday there between my many European tours. I always stay at the enchanting Hotel Cap Martin, and the view from my window over the big, sunny hotel-terrace to palm trees, flowers and blue sea is a cherished memory. I much prefer the path out of the bare cliff hard by the foaming sea than the famous terrace in front of the Casino: I find the terrible pigeon-shooting unbearable. It is a "sport" for which I have not a shadow of understanding. . . . The life and excitement of the Casino itself, after the first glamour wore off, held no attractions for me. Nor have I a passion for gambling. I never

173

knew the prewar Riviera, but I had imagined everything much more elegant and fashionable. And even here all traces of postwar depression have not entirely vanished. It reminds me of an aging beauty who makes up twice as heavily, loads herself with masses of glittering jewelry and says with a painful smile: "I am beautiful, I am elegant and desirable. Look at me! I am just the same as I used to be years ago. . . ." But one remembers with sorrow the time when she was young and beautiful and real and undefiled. . . .

I gladly escaped from the places of noisy entertainment which had no attractions for me; I preferred the gracious warmth of the southern sun and the blue silk of the sea on fine days, and the deep red of the cliffs in the evening light. . . .

I went into ecstasies of delight over the fairy-tale city of Venice. I shall never forget my first day there, the arrival at the railway station in front of which wait the slender, black gondolas, so that one can step out of the dull commonplace of every-day life, hurry through a lane of importunate, brightly clad porters, and there one is in a fairyland, sitting already in a gondola, with the beat of oars, the plashing of water and the old cry of the gondoliers . . . the tumult subsides. Old palaces on the banks, legendary, fragile, like ancient, yellowed ivory, lovely and fine . . . cracked marble, the split magnificence of fine costly brocade . . . Desdemona's palace. . . . And there, there is where Richard Wagner died, there lived and suffered the great, unforgettable Duse. . . . Oh, what a city! Gulls fly over the Grand Canal, and the in-

174

numerable pigeons, predatory, bold and greedy though they are, seem fabulous and unreal as they flutter in pale flocks among heedless stepping feet which the little thieves always contrive to dodge. Naturally I have a picture of myself—who wouldn't be photographed on St. Mark's Square with pigeons fluttering round? . . .

Venice in the rain: cheerless, dismal, like some ghostly nightmare . . . for that city, the sun is essential. In the rain it makes one weary of life. . . .

From the Lido I traveled by air for the first time in my life. We had an early swim in the sea—flew to Vienna in two and a half hours, and surprised my mother at afternoon coffee at Hinterbrühl. . . . So we sat and had coffee under the old chestnut tree, and I looked up at the white clouds over which we had floated just a few hours before, when they lay below us like a huge, gleaming snow field. . . .

CHAPTER
NINETEEN

IT HAD always been one of Franz Schalk's dearest wishes that I should sing Isolde. The part had a quite special attraction for me: I loved it with the stubborn tenacity of the unlucky in love. . . . I literally dreamed about it . . . I studied it by myself and wept with joy as over something forever unattainable. For my voice lacks the great dramatic power that must triumphantly defy the orchestra when the elemental drama breaks loose without harming itself.

Schalk often said to me: "If you could only be reasonable and restrain yourself, of course you could sing Isolde—perfectly well! You would just need to keep back and husband your voice. But do you really think you could do that?" . . . But that wasn't what I wanted at all, I wanted to enjoy it completely, to be able to act and sing that marvelous part without moderation or restraint . . . to lavish myself blissfully, entirely on Isolde. . . .

Then once, when I was telling Bruno Walter of this dream of my life he said: "One would have to conduct you very carefully, keep down the orchestra as much as possible and give you a not too heroic Tristan. Perhaps you'll do it with me in Berlin?"

It was a great temptation: Walter would spare my voice even more than Schalk, whose nature it was to get lost in sound; his joy in my singing would have communicated itself dangerously to me . . . whereas Walter would spare and restrain it and keep it carefully in hand. . . .

But how could I prepare Schalk for a disappointment—for I sincerely loved and admired him.

So I came to Vienna in a state of desperate indecision. . . .

The best way is the direct one! I made a sudden decision and told Schalk that I had a chance of singing Isolde in Berlin, and asked whether he would allow me to do it without feeling angry with me.

I can still see him sitting beside me at the piano in that unforgettable hour. "Under no conditions," he said most amiably, "would I like you to sing Isolde in Berlin first and not in Vienna where you belong. But I'll make you another suggestion. I shall invite Walter to conduct it for you here. . . ."

"No, I don't want that," I retorted immediately. "I know that you always wanted to do Isolde with me—and you know, I hope, how happy I am singing under you. . . ."

Schalk looked down at the keyboard over which his unusually beautiful hands absently strayed.

177

"No, dear Lotte, I am an old man—the rehearsals for your Fidelio affected me deeply—I don't know how I could bear your Isolde. . . ."

Never in all my life has anyone given me such a precious gift as Schalk did with those words, on which I look back with pride and emotion.

But Isolde remained an unfulfilled dream. My own judgment warned me against such a dangerous experiment. . . . For long I mourned her sorrowfully, but I found full compensation in wonderful lieder. Perhaps in that battle with the waves of orchestral sound Isolde would have lost for me that tender lyrical quality of voice necessary for lieder-singing. So I must be thankful that I did renounce her. Thankful, too, to my friend Melchior, the most famous Tristan of today, who warned me urgently against doing the part—and after a talk with him I finally gave up the idea of ever singing it. Leo Slezak actually wrote me a long letter when he heard of my plans, which absolutely horrified him. Slezak is always full of the most devastating humor. Even this letter bristled with jokes and sarcasms—but I read his concern for me in its none too tender words, and thanked my dear colleague from my heart for his honest friendship.

With ever greater inclination I fled to the magic kingdom of the lied. Lieder-recitals took me repeatedly to Belgium, Italy and France. I have sung at private concerts for nearly all the Rothschilds in Paris. The Parisians are very true to me. They prefer above anything simple, tender songs—

My Country House in Hinterbrühl, Near Vienna.

Schumann's "Nut-tree," for instance, is one of their favorites. The elegant, *mondaine* audience is most enthusiastic, and their devotion is touching. The memory will never fade of the day when France gave me the Legion of Honour: I sang the lieder illustrating a lecture on Beethoven by Barthou, who was then Prime Minister. Barthou, who was also a music scholar (he has written books on Beethoven and Wagner), had been one of my most faithful concert-goers ever since our Paris *Fidelio*. Soon there was a whole community of Lehmann admirers in Paris, who always gathered round me at all my recitals: Barthou, Painlévé, Herriot, Paul Clemenceau and his wife. And in the front row there always sat a very beautiful blonde young woman of whom I shall have more to say later.

It was a wonderful moment when, at the conclusion of his lecture Barthou again made a gesture to the enthusiastically applauding audience for silence. He said that by my art I had endeared myself to the hearts of French music-lovers, and that he had great pleasure in decorating me with the Order of the Legion of Honour. A wild outburst of cheering came from the whole hall! Barthou himself fastened the cross on my breast and kissed me "in the name of France." I was so moved and overcome that I could scarcely speak, and just stammered out *"Merci."* . . . And the enchanting Barthou remarked amiably to the audience with a smile: *"Elle est absolument charmante. Je l'embrace et elle me remercie."* . . .

Very few foreign women possess the Legion of Honour.

179

It is a decoration I wear with special pride. What a pity my dear father didn't live to witness this great joy!

The months I spent in Vienna became fewer and fewer. . . . Of modern operas I sang Korngold's Heliane, his Marietta in the *Toten Stadt,* in which rôle Maria Jeritza had conquered the audience of the Metropolitan; then Blanchefleur in Kienzl's *Kuhreigen,* Don Gil in Braunfels' *Don Gil von den Grünen Hosen,* Luise in Zajicek-Blankenau's *Ferdinand und Luise*—this most melodious opera is dedicated to my dear friend, Countess Gabi Rechberg. *Intermezzo* came, of course, to Vienna too, and I was partnered by the incomparable Jerger. In *Ariadne* I had exchanged the charming rôle of the Composer for that of Ariadne herself. Of Italian parts, I sang Tosca, Desdemona, Mimi, Butterfly, Madeleine and Manon. My repertoire of lieder soon comprehended a heavenly profusion of the loveliest gems of its literature. I frequently sang at home to a close circle of friends at lovely intimate evenings—and I remember one New Year's Eve when we sang the entire ensemble from the act of *Lohengrin* with Carl Alwin at the piano; Maria Olszewska as Ortrude; myself as Elsa; Schmedes, Lohengrin; Schipper, Telrasmund; and Muzzarelli, König Heinrich. . . . And then Lucie Weidt and Schmedes sank the duet from *Gotterdammerung*—and we listened with emotion to the voice of an artist who had already "retired," that reminded us of lovely, unforgettable performances. How they were feted and cheered, Schmedes and the grandiose Lucie Weidt!

180

I must not forget my concert tour to Athens. I spent one lovely day there and have hardly ever met with such genuine and open hospitality. Everyone wanted to show me something new and they all outvied one another in kindness. I stayed at a house that contains the largest and most valuable collection of Byzantine art in the world. I stood on the Parthenon in warm sunlight that made the pink-gold marble shimmer as if it were suffused with rosy blood. I stood by the temple of Poseidon and looked down on the Aegean Sea—over me the deep blue sky of Greece. . . .

The only sad thing is the people's lack of sympathy for animals.

"The animal has no soul," they say; and the noble lady who founded the Society for the Protection of Animals has to struggle hard against deep-rooted prejudices. I myself constantly saw those helpless creatures of God being ill-treated, and my dreams are often haunted by the hunted look in the eyes of the poor homeless dog that I tried in vain to call to me. . . . Those things were the only shadows on the sunny days at Athens. . . . Venizelos, then president, came to my concerts and I had the pleasure of making his acquaintance; his marvelous basket of roses went with me to Vienna as the last token of all the beauty and appreciation I had found in Athens.

CHAPTER
TWENTY

YEARS before, I had already received a contract from the Chicago Civic Opera, but it was of the Metropolitan that I dreamed as the crown of my operatic career. . . . It was a long time, however, before they decided to engage me. My name was already famous throughout Europe—and still the Metropolitan remained passive. . . .

In the *Frau ahne Schatten* the demoniac nurse sings: "Supernatural powers are at work. . . ." What mighty powers I had to contend with there, I have no idea. . . .

In any case I accepted, after long hesitation, a repeated offer from Chicago in 1930—really only because I wanted to see America. . . . My dear mother was quite horrified at my wanting to go to the "New World." So I promised her that as long as she lived, which I hoped would be for many, many years, that I would only spend a few weeks "passing through," and so being over there would not separate me any longer from her than my European concert tours. All the same it was a sad parting. The thought that the great ocean would stretch between me and my "home" had still

182

all the terror of novelty for me. South America and my violent homesickness there were still fresh in my memory. . . . My husband accompanied me—not for anything would I have gone alone. Maria Olszewska, Frieda Leider, Eduard Habig and Pollak the conductor, were traveling to the Chicago engagement at the same time. In Paris there was a hasty farewell concert, and at Cherbourg we went on board the *Europa*. What a terrific experience! To go aboard that brightly lit, enormous floating hotel for the first time is a breath-taking sensation. . . . As it happened there was little time for journeys of exploration: as soon as we left Cherbourg we ran into a bad storm. It was the worst I have ever experienced on an ocean voyage. The enormous ship was tossed about like a ball on the waves, and we lay in our cabins, wretched and indifferent. For two days the hurricane raged, and when we gradually reappeared on the promenade deck, we all looked pale and exhausted as if we had gone through a severe illness. But the rest of the voyage was wonderful and richly compensated us for the suffering we had endured.

New York emerged from morning mist—a gigantic Fata Morgana, a visionary Valhalla beyond the clouds and shimmering sea. . . .

The tiresome business of the customs on the quay . . . the sleeves of Elsa's robe was searched for tobacco and Elisabeth's nun's hood for whisky and cognac—for this was 1930, and there was still strict prohibition!

183

First impressions of the bustle of New York life: cars and cars. . . . One sat in a car, feeling slightly dazed with the noise and the gigantic crowds all around. . . . The sky-scrapers were oppressive. The humming lift that took us up in the Savoy Plaza let us out at the twenty-eighth floor! . . . It made one dizzy to look out of the window. . . . I felt like a peasant coming to the city for the first time—in spite of London and Paris. . . .

The next day: the Grand Central Station. Good Heavens— and what a station! It is more like a palace! Marble, bronze . . . no one in a hurry. Nobody rushes about excitedly with bags. Everything is discreetly arranged. After a long walk through the tunnel we got into the train—to right and to left of us the steel colossus of the railway car. The attendants, all negroes, stand at the doors in shining white jackets, ready with the most courteous service. We had a drawing room, a proper comfortable little room with a private lavatory. Every coach has its drawing room, and the rest of the passengers sleep in artfully constructed beds which during the day are transformed into comfortable sofas like those in the drawing rooms. Men and women sleep together in one car but the beds are so marvelously separated by tightly drawn curtains that there is no fear of any indiscretions. The beds are thoroughly comfortable, broad and scrupulously clean. There is ample washing accommodation for men and women in every car. There is no stinting of linen:

124

whole piles of snow-white hand towels lie ready in the lavatory, and the attendant wraps one's coat in huge sheets. I christened all the negroes "Mohrchen," and since then all my friends in America call them that. . . . The attendant Mohrchens are all specially chosen good and trustworthy people, all most courteous, helpful and obliging. They are incredibly precisely drilled: in the dining car every movement is mechanical like some well-functioning machine. . . . The tablecloths are changed for every guest, and it is a joy to watch how speedily a table is laid again, with a flashing of glasses, cutlery and snowy linen. The Mohrchens all look as if they had just come out of a soapy bath. Against their dark-glowing skin their black fuzzy hair lies like comic woolly mops, their clean white jackets make their heads and hands look duskier than ever.

My first trip to the United States was a real adventure for me, full of surprises and thrills. . . .

Chicago! The Drake Hotel on Lake Michigan . . . a wonderful view from the hotel building over the boundless expanse of water. . . . The lake is bigger than the North Sea, but it is mostly very gloomy, gray-black enveloped in mist. . . . The enormous motor road alongside is like the Promenade des Anglais in Nice—on an enormous scale. A succession of moving cars forms a never-ending chain. In the evening the lights, like brilliants, are ranged in broad, shining bands. . . . Somewhere out there lie the Chicago slaughter-

185

houses which supply nearly the whole of America with meat. . . . Somewhere out there long trains roll up with thousands of animals, driven dumb and helpless to their fate. . . . On the trucks is already written up in big letters: "Excellent ham, first-class bacon." . . . They are still alive, but they have already become "meat," divided-up goods, they are already delicacies ready to be eaten. . . .

It is foolish to let one's mind dwell on those inevitabilities of life. . . .

The Civic Opera is a huge commercial building with shops and offices. . . . Among other things they sell music there—very good music too; under Egon Pollak we gave very fine performances. The stage is fitted with the most modern devices. The dressing rooms have their own bathrooms. There is a slight defect about the auditorium: the boxes are all at the back on one tier, and the elegant occupants are far away from the stage and—what is more important!—have a very bad view of the audience, and are seen very little themselves. . . . The wonderful clothes, valuable jewelry and heavenly furs—why wear those at the Opera where no one sees them properly? The audience of the Chicago boxes is dissatisfied with the opera house. . . .

I don't know how it is, but I have never found any place where it is so draughty as at the entrances of this opera house. . . . Wherever you open a door, you set up a wild wind that ruffles your hair, tears at your clothes and hurls you

186

right back if it catches you unawares, so that when you finally pantingly manage to close the door behind you, you look as if you had just escaped from a free fight.

At first I suffered terribly from the overheated dressing rooms. It is a remarkable thing about that country—the unbearable waste of fuel everywhere. The cost of coal seems to be of no consequence. So the hotels and apartment houses are always overheated. Even the walls are warm. . . . I scarcely ever turn on the heating in my rooms, and my first step in every hotel is to the window—to let in fresh air and the cool of the morning. And then suddenly a murderous cold that pierces to the marrow will set in. This land of "unlimited possibilities" seems to deal only in superlatives—even in the matter of climatic changes. Sometimes you go out into the close atmosphere of a hothouse; then suddenly an icy wind sweeps unexpectedly round a street corner and you come home in a snowstorm for which the wild and romantic name of "blizzard" is so suitable. . . . In Chicago I have known such terribly cold days that no fur was any protection. Stormy Lake Michigan with its raging waves would freeze over and make the beach with the congealed mountainous masses a grotesque sight. In front of the hotel entrances in storm, rain or snow, they put up tentlike shelters across the pavement to the street so that one can flee to one's car with a certain measure of protection. I remember one short, violent spell of cold in Chicago which I transformed into an illusion of summer: after my husband left I stayed at

187

Chicago's big clubhouse, the Women's Athletic Club. My friend Mia from Atlanta was staying with me for a time, and we spent all my free hours in the marvelous swimming pool. There it was warm, light and pleasant; we sat on chaises-lounges in our swimming suits, drank tea, did exercises in the big gymnasium, swam in the magnificent pool and forgot winter, cold and blizzard. . . .

My trip to America that year and the following one only lasted a few weeks. Real successes are not enough to set one's feet firmly in America—I mean to make one really popular. More than anywhere else one needs an actual sensation to start one on a proper career. I sang and had excellent press notices. But not for a moment was there the glamour surrounding my person and my art that is essential for a "world-star." In Minneapolis I gave a lieder-recital without making any special impression. My New York Manager, Mr. Coppicus, with whom I had made a contract for several concerts before I came to Chicago, postponed my intended New York recital to 1932. Coppicus had heard me in Paris, had of course expected a repetition of the Paris enthusiasm, and so was rather disappointed. I myself inwardly agreed with him. . .

"I'm not for America," I thought, "however, we shall see. . . ." I readily postponed the concerts and would just as readily have canceled my contract with him if he had wanted. For in no other profession are contracts built on such unsure foundations as in ours: what manager, what theater director

188

can compel an artist? Art is not a commodity. We must give from our whole soul what we have to give, otherwise we would not be artists. A "performance" that is in any way compelled and given ungladly can scarcely be a success. And what is the use of the most marvelous contract if we are found wanting, if the concerts are empty, if the audience doesn't want us? We ourselves won't want to fulfill the contract in that case. So I left everything to the future and went back to Vienna with the honest consciousness of having had a good average success in Chicago—nothing more. . . .

CHAPTER
TWENTY-ONE

SCHALK, after ten years' office as director—not counting the two years he shared the directorate with Strauss— had retired. Too many people wanted to have a hand in running the Opera. . . . The very ambitious general manager Schneiderhan also meddled in artistic matters which, to Schalk's mind, were not in his province. Schalk, always gentlemanly, smooth and elegant, was no fighter. Constant misunderstandings, interference with his rights and vexations from all sides exhausted his strength and weakened his naturally delicate health. So he gave it up . . . but I can imagine that it was no easy renunciation for him, for no one had loved the Opera House, had served it and given it strength and life as he had. It must have grieved him to leave that room, to rise from that great desk where he had spent innumerable hours, working untiringly. . . .

He neither wanted nor needed to resign from conducting as well. So he stayed on with us under the title, specially created for him by the Opera House, of General Director of Music, when the new head, Clemens Krauss, took up his duties. With him came a new world. Krauss brought a whole staff of new singers with him, and probably wouldn't have minded if all the others had vanished from the scene. An impressive personality, he stuck to his friends with tenacious obduracy, worked for them and exposed himself for their sakes!

The Vienna Opera grew strange to me. I fled more and more to foreign countries. But the Viennese people remained true to me. Whenever I sang—in the Opera or at lieder-recitals—I was overwhelmed with a warm wave of love and friendship. It was as if they wanted to keep telling this faithlessly faithful one: "You belong to us. We love you. We understand you. . . ." It was this period in particular that made me doubly attached to Vienna. . . .

After his secession Schalk's health began to fail. Since the concentrated work had been taken from him he seemed to become crippled and weak. Like a phantom of the past his slight, fragile form glided through the corridors, but he always hurried past the door that had once led to his own domain. . . . I have a photograph of him taken during this, his last period, that I cannot look on unmoved, so deep is the amazement of his expression, the amazement and aversion, as if he were looking on a world he no longer understood. . . . In June, 1931, I sang for the last time with him—in *Ariadne*. He was already very ill and sometimes it seemed as if his arms had not the strength to obey his will. Then came one last *Tristan,* and it seemed as if he had regained his old fire,

191

as if his whole will had been revived again at the sacred flame—so well did he raise this performance to wonted heights. He was tremendously acclaimed, and the too-slender form at the desk bent under the storm of applause. Then something very strange happened: Schalk remained standing at his desk until the whole house had emptied. He had folded his hands on the parapet that separates the orchestra from the audience, and embraced the whole of the great, beautiful old building in a loving look. Was it a premonition of his approaching end? Was he taking a sorrowful farewell of the abodes to which his whole heart belonged? Who knows. . . . A tired man, broken and doomed to death, he was the last to leave the building. . . .

I visited him toward the end of June at the Baden Sanatorium before I left for my summer holiday in Sylt. He had altered tremendously: his face had lost all its sharpness, as though a gentle hand had passed over it with a beautifying and transfiguring touch. . . . His eyes, free of all sarcasm, shone with an unearthly light, and his hair, which had grown quite white, waved more richly on his high, intellectual forehead. I valiantly fought my tears and sought for a word that would please him.

"I have decided to do Isolde after all," I said with an effort, "and you must promise me you'll let me do *Tristan* with you in Autumn."

His lovely hand stroked mine feebly.

"It is too late," he said in a soft, tired voice. . . .

192

—*Foto-Kolhmaier*, Salzburg

Lotte Lehmann and Bruno Walter Take a Bow after Their Joint Lieder Recital.

It was too late: on September 3, 1931, his eyes closed forever. It was not granted to me to see him again. I could only follow his coffin when, according to his wishes, he was borne to his last rest in the simple little mountain churchyard at Reichenau. Hundreds of people were not prevented from coming from Vienna to accompany him on his last journey. The upright form of his wife walked behind the coffin of her beloved life's companion, and her bearing, as she climbed the steep little path to his grave, had the moving dignity of frozen and ecstatic sorrow.

I had to sing Eva that evening. . . . Krauss had met my refusal with the very proper objection: "Do you think that the deceased would have wanted you to put the Opera into difficulties? . . ." That certainly was not the case . . . so I sang.

From the State Opera House hung the long black flag, and before the beginning of the Opera the funeral march from *Gotterdämmerung* was played in memory of Franz Schalk.

For me it only became a true occasion of mourning when in the last act the chorus "Awake!" recalled to my mind the familiar figure at the desk. . . . I closed my eyes, and it was as if he were there again—surrendered to the waves of music: "Awake! The dawn of day draws near. . . ." An uncontrollable fit of weeping shook me, and my colleagues quickly formed a protecting wall round me so that no one might see my tears. . . .

193

Incidentally the summer holidays that had just ended were the first really adequate and proper rest I had had for a long time. I had turned down the Salzburg performances because I did not want to spend my very precious free time in the changed atmosphere there. . . . Only toward the end of the Festival did I come to Salzburg to give a lieder-recital with Bruno Walter. Ten weeks' holiday had made me more avid for work than I had almost ever been—no studying of lieder could make up for my customary strenuous activity. From my long daily rides over the Sylt moors I was burned a deep brown by sun and wind. Nevertheless, I was very surprised to be greeted at Salzburg with joyful amazement by all my acquaintances: "So you're better now? Thank Heaven you've recovered!"

"Recovered? What do you mean?"

"Weren't you very ill? I heard you were. . . ."

Then an embarrassed silence. . . .

Gradually I learned that the wildest rumors had been busied with my unusually long holidays—the mildest being that I was sinking fast from some hopeless lung trouble at Davos. And of course I had divorced my husband. . . . It created quite a sensation when we appeared at Salzburg together. . . .

194

CHAPTER
TWENTY-TWO

AT THE beginning of January, 1933, I went back to America. But before I set off for Chicago, my New York recital that had been planned two years before, took place at last. My manager Coppicus was surprised that the recital was practically sold out: he had perhaps underestimated my popularity in Europe, the result of many concerts and festival-performances at which countless Americans had heard me at Salzburg and in London and Paris. Of course I was known only to those wealthy music-lovers who make a yearly pilgrimage to Europe to enjoy art, and, above all, music. To the great public I was entirely unknown. Mr. Coppicus told me that he had heard reports that several people at the booking office had asked with suspicious surprise: "But Lehmann must have died long ago? She is simply ancient. . . . She sang at the Metropolitan several decades ago!" Then it was explained that this new singer was Lotte and not Lilli. . . .

I came to the United States alone. My husband was prevented from coming with me—and I felt horribly lonely in that enormous city. If only I knew that one friend, one sympathetic soul was to be in the hall! This first concert was to determine my concert career in America. New York is the focal-point of interest. Whoever conquers there finds all doors open to him. . . . I spent the whole afternoon before my recital nervously and feverishly pacing up and down my room. I gave a fleeting thought to the lovely young woman who had always sat in the front row at all my Paris recitals: would she keep her word and come? It had been a remarkable experience for me: I had noticed her in Paris because her very mobile and expressive face had always been transformed, while I sang, to an ecstasy of rapturous surrender, so that I often had the feeling that I was singing for this strange woman to whom my singing apparently meant something quite special. She was always accompanied by a tall, slim, very young man. I often asked my friends about about her, but nobody knew her. Then one day I received a wonderful bouquet of flowers and a letter in English in which a stranger thanked me for all my recitals which she had so much enjoyed. She had now to return with her husband to her home in America, but if I ever gave a recital in New York, she would be there with her husband in the front row. . . . I wired to the ship she was sailing by—for I felt something akin to gratitude toward her: she had given me such stimulation by the devotion to my voice she had disclosed, that I felt indebted to her and wanted very much to make her acquaintance.

196

Now, alone in New York, I had an ardent desire to find the familiar face of this unknown in the strange audience again.

Shaken with nerves and only half-conscious, I stepped from the threshold of the artists' room on to the platform of the Town Hall.

I was greeted, quite unexpectedly, by welcoming applause that lasted for several minutes.

Lots of the people in the hall must know me, many must love me and be glad to see me in New York! And I had thought I was going to appear before an audience that expected "someone new." . . . And there—in the front row— was the lovely face of my unknown friend! Suddenly I was no longer alone. . . . The storm of applause had delivered me from my bonds of fear, and I sang the whole evening through as if I were drunk with happiness, ecstasy and jubilant triumph! Oh, and it was a triumph! I have no intention of bragging about my successes in this book, but this first New York recital was tremendously important for my whole career in America, and I simply can't pass over it in two words. The audience became as ecstatic as myself—there was a constant give and take—and it was only after many recalls and encores that I had at last to make an end. . . .

My Parisian unknown hurried round to me, overwhelmed by the success. She took me weeping in her arms—and, incidentally, since then she has become a dear friend of mine, although she struggled tremendously against getting to know

197

me "properly." But perhaps it wasn't so bad knowing Lotte Lehmann the person as well as the artist? . . . Mr. Coppicus, of course, was radiant at my success. He had hardly expected it—certainly not to that extent. . . .

"Did you see how Geraldine Farrar applauded you?"

"Oh Heavens, no! Where was she sitting?"

He described the place and I certainly had seen the conspicuously beautiful, elegant woman with the gray hair and incredibly bright eyes without knowing that it was the Farrar I had raved about as a student in Berlin. . . . I sent her a telegram that night. Cables were dispatched to my people in Vienna. And as I lay in bed in the Chicago train, I could have gone on singing with joy and high spirits.

After the Chicago season—which again lasted only a few weeks for me—I gave a "farewell recital" in New York the day I left for home, for which every available seat was sold. The concert began at 3 P.M.—in America those recitals start at quite extraordinary times—my boat sailed at 6 o'clock, and opposite the platform was a clock whose hands I watched anxiously between my songs. . . . Encore after encore prolonged the recital interminably, and at last I had to say to my audience: "I should like to sing you lots more songs, but my boat won't wait. . . ." I went on board with a contract for a long concert tour in my pocket, and my only worry was how my dear mother would take it if I left her longer than I had intended and promised. . . . Mamma lived from spring to autumn in her house at Hinterbrühl, tended by her good

Marie, without whom her life would have been practically unthinkable. In the winter I had taken a nice, comfortable flat for her very near my house in town; my brother devoted all his free time to her, so she was always well taken care of. My brother had lost his wife through a cruel, lingering illness, had devoted himself to nursing her with all the generosity of his impulsive nature, and now, after her death, was plunged into the misery of sudden loneliness. He found a new incentive in his pupils and I was tremendously glad when he was appointed teacher of operatic drama at that excellent music school, the New Vienna Conservatoire. Whenever he was free he lavished all his devotion and love on our mother. So I could stay away for longer without really worrying—all the more so since my good mother-in-law wanted to spend a few weeks at our house in Vienna. But I had a bad conscience, and the thought that, at the Christmas tree, Mamma would shed one tear, not of joy but of longing, made me quite miserable. I was in a state of terrible indecision. The world called me, the wide world that seemed to have no more limits for me. . . .

I can still see my mother standing at the garden gate as I said good-by to her in late autumn, for the first time for several months . . . her dear good old face streaming with tears . . . beside her, her inseparable companion, the little Pomeranian Mohrle who had grown old with her and was pledged to his mistress for life and death . . . and on the other side her "adopted dog," my lovely little Maltese Pizzi,

199

who was to remain in her charge while we were away. . . . I cried a great deal and was greatly grieved at this parting, but a wide unknown world lay before me and I wanted to conquer it and win its devotion, so my eyes although dimmed with tears, looked forward and no longer backward. . . . When I think today how many partings my beloved old mamma had to endure, how often the excitement of happy reunions alternated with heartbreaking farewells, I often doubt whether I was the good daughter I meant to be to her, and that she deserved. Of course, I was able to fulfill all her wishes and make the twilight of her life a happy one, but perhaps she would have been happier living a peaceful, bourgeois life in a humble little home with her daughter, without all this coming and going of which my life now consisted. I cannot think without regret of all the tears she shed for me at our partings. . . .

My first big concert tour was full of thrills. We traveled through the length and breadth of America. Since then my permanent accompanist in America has been Ernö Balogh, a Hungarian by birth who had been naturalized as an American for some considerable time. In the many concerts I have sung with him, he has been the faithful and understanding companion of my artistic intentions. He is also a really sincerely devoted friend, helpful and always with my interests at heart. It was a good thing for us that we had a traveling companion on this first tour who already knew the land well. For it was full of surprises for us. Typical is the American

200

manager's way of putting it, not "I have arranged these concerts for you," but "I have sold you for such and such for this concert,"—an avowal that irritated me to tears at first. . . . It was difficult to accustom oneself to the tempo. Two things one must never say in America, "I am tired," and "I don't feel well." . . . It is a hard business learning that cruel, but, at the same time, incredibly self-disciplining expression: "Keep smiling." . . . People often ask me what the American audience is like—to which I cannot possibly give a comprehensive answer. It is absolutely different and always unexpected: often in smaller towns one comes across an astonishing degree of appreciation of the German lied, often one has the depressing feeling of singing to bare, dead walls. . . . Then it is always like a battle: I vow obstinately to myself that I will conquer them—that I will trap them in the net of lieder I will cast over them. . . . Sometimes I don't succeed. Then I am as exhausted as if I had been through the hardest physical labor. In many towns I sing in four languages. Many artists tour America with only one program and sing the same one for weeks. That would drive me mad. Of course, I do not make life any easier by singing different programs, but for me singing is not only a way of earning money and gaining fame, it is a part of my life, the finest and best part . . . and I want to enjoy singing for its own sake.

It makes me happy when I can choose really good programs. On the other hand one must learn to recognize the various grades of musical understanding. Vienna, of course, is a musical city of high culture, built on the foundations of a golden tradition. In America they are building up a tradition for future generations. In Europe we pluck the fruit, in America we foster and cherish the tree which will one day bear the fruit. . . . In many parts of America it is pioneer work, awakening the appreciation of the lied. Naturally, one cannot expect a musically uneducated audience to listen with interest to a whole evening of unknown songs in a strange language. So one has to give a mixed program, and sing English songs they are familiar with. Then an interposed group of German lieder is sure of a friendly welcome, for they will say: "A voice that has given pleasure in well-known songs in our language, will now sing a group of her own national songs. They are beautiful too. . . ."

Of course I am only speaking of one part of the audience. There are towns with a European appreciation of music, not to mention New York which is, of course, entirely cosmopolitan, very spoiled, and tremendously critical.

For me it is still today just as thrilling as ever to face a new audience: will it understand and take me to its heart? It is rather like an exciting puzzle. But on my first concert tour I suffered under it.

I was surprised at coming across relatively few reporters. In travel descriptions, novels and interviews one reads so much about the aggressiveness of the press. Balogh explained to me that any artist on tour who wants to make proper

202

capital out of his successes must have a special press-manager—a so-called "personal representative." I was horrified at the thought.

"What, all that must be arranged and paid for?" I cried indignantly, "all this publicity and those pictures in the papers—that is done by arrangement instead of the press taking an interest of its own accord? Never in my life will I do that."

"But you simply don't understand this country," Balogh explained, "it is so enormously big. Who knows anything about you and your European successes here? A tiny percentage of this huge republic. To the rest you are completely unknown. Your name must be repeated over and over again throughout the whole country so that it sticks in their minds, and only in this way can you become really well known. There are about two thousand towns in America where you can give concerts. But it is not enough here to sing. You must become well known in all sorts of ways, through publicity stories that would seem stupid to you, but nevertheless have their importance. . . ."

"Never," I declared violently, "I will do nothing inartistic and I think it is most inartistic to advertise myself. I will conquer by singing. But not otherwise. . . ."

Balogh was silent, and his skeptical smile made me very annoyed.

I learned much later how right he was, as I will duly relate.

203

Meanwhile, it was hard enough to say with a smile that I felt as fresh as a daisy when I stepped out of the train dead tired, and was met by a delegation of clubwomen or managers at the station. . . . It was difficult after a recital to have to sign hundreds of autographs patiently, hurry off to the station in my concert gown, frequently with almost nothing to eat but a sandwich in a drugstore. These drugstores are a marvelous American institution; originally intended as a sort of chemist's shop, they finally became a place where you can buy all sorts of unexpected things; they are open day and night, and you can buy, in addition to every kind of medicine, clocks, perfume, traveling requisites, stationery and umbrellas, electrical fittings and children's toys. . . . In the middle of the day you can even get a cheap lunch there, and there are always sandwiches to be had and those wonderful refreshing drinks whose variety and subtle flavors are a product of prohibition: various "milk shakes," mixtures of excellent milk, cream, vanilla ice cream and some mysterious extra dash. To save time, for "time is money," everything is electrically mixed; an electric "freezer" is dipped into the beaker, buzzing and hissing like a freezing stroke of lightning—and in one minute the drink is ready, served up in a paper container. . . .

I was amazed at the long cheerless desolate expanses the express rushed through. Accustomed to the changing scenes of the European landscapes, woods, fields, villages and pleasant towns, I now saw to the right and to the left of the railway

204

track the same thing for hours on end—bare fields, magnificent motor roads, service stations, towns all built to the same pattern, functional and completely lacking in feeling, as if the inhabitants had said to themselves: "Who knows how long I'll live here. Perhaps in a year I'll find better living conditions elsewhere. Meanwhile let us dump ourselves here. . . ." No time to make the house look a little nicer . . . nor is there any time to arrange the graveyards with any reverence: it looks as if the dead had been buried in a hurry. . . . The graveyards have no walls, and very few of the graves are decorated with flowers.

The women spend a great deal of time in "make-up" and grooming. The "beauty shops" are always packed. The name is significant. There one can buy beauty. . . . In all the stores one scarcely ever comes across a shopgirl who is not very carefully made up and manicured. Not to mention the fact that they have platinum-blonde or chestnut "perms" according to the prevailing fashion!

On our very first tour we went to California. The way through the desert was impressive in its aridness. Incredible is the marvelous motor road that crosses the entire desert, broad and perfect, with the indispensable service stations as a constant commemoration to a hustling age. . . . We paid a short visit to an Indian village by getting into a Cook's motor-coach that was waiting at Albuquerque and rushing off at all possible speed to the Indian reservation, where for about twenty minutes we watched native Indian dances arranged

205

by Cook's. We shuddered at the magnificent eagle faces, that look as if they were carved in bronze, of this proud, dying savage race, and then rushed back by coach to catch the impatiently puffing train already awaiting us at the next station. . . . The mohrchens shout their "All aboard" that sounds like "oooupp," we hurry into our carriages and already we are off again. It is a four nights' and three days' journey from New York to Los Angeles. With the small matter of an extra half-day thrown in, you can see one of the greatest wonders of the world—the Grand Canyon in Colorado. Luckily we did have time for this short excursion. And while our train flew on through the desert waste our carriage was attached to a cable railway, and we woke up in the morning 6000 feet up in deep snow. The Grand Canyon is difficult to describe: it is the deepest ravine in the world and bewilderingly and overwhelmingly beautiful. The formation of the rocky walls is unusual; they are like artificially constructed pillared halls with archways, altars, and huge heads of petrified gods. . . . The stone shimmers with a fantastic irridescence: a delicate pink alternating with deep blue and mauve. . . . It makes one speechless to look down 6000 feet into the ravine—from the midst of ice and snow into this petrified realm of enchantment. It looks as though an enormous meteor might have fallen from the sky and, still burning, bored its way into the bowels of the earth, and its fires have stained the walls those bright colors that neither wind nor rain nor sun can erase . . . so powerfully and precipitately does the earth seem to have been torn up here by cosmic forces. . .

Los Angeles, to which I had been looking forward so much was, at the time of our first visit, ravaged by a severe wave of influenza. In the train, shortly before we arrived, I was already shivering with fever—so I did not see much of Los Angeles: I lay seriously ill in the lovely Ambassador Hotel, and only saw the giant palms through the window, and flowering creepers on the trellis work of the balcony—and a great deal of warm radiant sunlight. It was December. I had to put off my recitals, but it was almost miraculous how quickly I recovered in the warm sun.

I found one friend in Hollywood, Lily Petschnikoff, the wife of the famous violinist, who lives near the Bowl with her son Sergei, who is, of course engaged in film work. The Bowl is an "open-air concert hall" that holds about 40,000 people, wherein summer fantastic performances are given, concerts with great conductors like Walter, Klemperer, etc. A few steps away is the little old house of the Petschnikoffs which constantly echoes with laughter. . . . Lily, who today is still a lovely woman with aristocratic features, flashing blue eyes and wild white locks, bubbles over with temperament and energy. She has two ancient residents, her ninety-four-year-old mother and her eighty-nine-year-old aunt. Both of them are local celebrities. They have one passion—motoring. . . . And Lily has always got to take them with her wherever she goes. . . . Often they are parked when Lily

207

has errands to do and there they sit, sometimes for a long time among hundreds of parked cars, and wait patiently. . . . Every parking attendant knows them and greets them with customary American familiarity: "Hello, old goils, how are you?" and puts the car at the street side so that the two old ladies have something to look at while they wait. . . .

Lily took me on my first walks after my convalescence through Hollywood, Pasadena, Santa Monica and Beverly Hills. I saw the palaces of the film stars, palms and magnificent flowers and streets compared to which the famous Promenade des Anglais is a little bare back-street. . . .

Concerts in wonderful San Francisco, Oakland and Sacramento—and then Christmas holidays! . . . A few lovely free days. . . . My husband and I spent them at Santa Barbara, an enchanting spot on the quiet ocean between San Francisco and Los Angeles. It was quite unChristmassy according to our ideas, even though everywhere huge Christmas trees stood in front of the houses, sumptuously decorated and lit up by hundreds of electric candles.

The big stores have even "engaged" good old Santa Claus, a brother of our German Father Christmas, for sales propaganda: he stands at the entrance doors in a bright-red suit trimmed with white fur, looking slightly "Russian" with his high boots, wide hood and long white beard. . . . He has a bell in his hand which he rings to encourage you to go in. Sometimes he sits in the window among children's toys, calling the attention of the little ones who are flattening their

noses on the panes outside to some specially tempting bar-
gain, so that many a mother finds great difficulties in satisfying all the new desires that Santa Claus has awakened in
her child. . . . Some shops have a Santa Claus consulting
department; one goes through fantastically decorated corridors to where Santa sits, gorgeously enthroned. The children line up in long queues, and I have often gone with
them in spite of "the terrible crush," because I find the quiver-
ing excitement of the little creatures so fascinating. There
are whispers and sighs and hesitating advances. . . . And
then at last they stand before the silvery throne; all around
silver-gauze clouds hang from a blue silk sky, stars shine at
the end of long threads, it has been snowing glittering cotton
wool, there are gaily-decked Christmas trees everywhere—
and oh! there is Santa Claus! It is a child's dream come true.
Santa holds out his arms and draws the shy ones toward him,
or playfully threatens the cheeky ones. . . . They whisper their
wishes in his ear, and to everything he nods assent. . . . Oh,
this Santa Claus must never say no—to good or bad alike. . . .

I was back in the old mysterious fairy-tale world of the
merry blessed Christmas time—but it vanished as I emerged
into the warm summer sunshine, with flowers blooming
and blossoming everywhere. . . . We breakfasted on the terrace of our bungalow in the charming Hotel Samarkand in
the warm sun, we rode for hours through the wild eucalyptus
forests past fields glowing red with poinsettias, and on the
broad, firm snow-white shore by the side of the sea. We

had wonderful horses, sat on cowboy saddles, and came back at midday quite sunburned. It didn't seem at all like Christmas. The little tree we had decorated brought no melancholy mood with it, for by the time it was lit, it was long past Christmas Eve "at home" in Vienna.

We also went to Canada on this tour. I sang at Winnipeg, and after all the masses of California flowers, the bitter cold which reaches forty degrees below freezing point—was twice as hard to bear. One would need an iron constitution to be able to stand these climatic changes without injuring one's health. One can hardly imagine the cold of Winnipeg—it is one of the coldest towns in Canada—that pierces to the very bone. I had to turn back when I started on my usual walk—I simply couldn't stand it!

At Buffalo, we saw the Niagara Falls half-frozen by the severe cold, a sight of grandiose and bizarre beauty. We saw a spring of burning water, in which one can dip a glass which seems to become filled with light blue flame—a wonder of Nature from which the Indians are supposed to have fled in panic when they first found the spring. But the congealed mass of the Niagara Falls seemed no less wonderful and awesome to me. A piercing wind soon drove us away, and we were quite glad to get into our warm train again and be borne off to New York, where we had taken up residence in a beautiful apartment hotel near Central Park.

With a song-recital as the artistic climax, I brought my first great American tour to an end.

210

CHAPTER
TWENTY-THREE

M Y MOTHER'S health was failing fast. She was approaching her eighty-third birthday, and she who had always been tortured by the fear of death, now longed for it as a deliverance from a life which had become a burden. Mohrle, the beloved little dog she had been so tenderly attached to, had died; she mourned for him as for some lost and irreplaceable friend—it even seemed as if the death of this faithful little companion had made her feel quite lonely. I have films taken of my mother in this last period of her life which reproduce her beloved image with affecting realism. I see, smiling down on me from the screen, that face etched with great age, grief and much bodily suffering, I see that mouth, now mute forever, speaking words that have died away, and that delicate, frail form coming up the garden path to me at our house at Hinterbrühl. . . . My mother-in-law stands beside her, a few years younger than she, full of life and vigor. The faithful Hinterbrühl doctor, Dr. Gerhard, smiles at my mother, there are flowers everywhere—the door to the veranda is festooned with garlands—the presents are

211

waiting. But the life that is celebrated here, surrounded by love and care, was nearing its close. . . . The flame was flickering that here still faintly burns. . . . A few weeks after her birthday, Mamma moved to her town flat. I had given her a new little Mohrle, just like the one that died, and it was one of her last pleasures.

At that time I had a great many rehearsals: Richard Strauss's *Arabella* was to be given in Vienna for the first time. At his request I was to have sung at the first performance at Dresden in June, but had to decline owing to overfatigue after the heavy season. Now I found in *Arabella* an interesting new task. Clemens Krauss conducted—and I can well say that the period when I was rehearsing with him is one of the most ungratifying recollections of my whole stage career. I am sure he would have preferred it if the singer who took my place at Dresden had done the Vienna *première* as well.

Every day, after those exhausting, nerve-racking rehearsals I went to my mother, who was becoming more and more transparent and was racked with pains. My husband would sit with her for hours every day, patient and full of sympathy and solicitude. My brother went to her whenever he was free—but all our love could no longer bring back her joy of life. . . .

I will not go into detail about those dark and sorrowful days. My beloved mother died the day after the dress-rehearsal of *Arabella*.

212

Lotte Lehmann, Lauritz Melchior and Mrs. Melchior.

For many years I had trembled at the thought of that terrible hour, and believed that I would never be able to endure that unbearable event. And now I stood by her deathbed and deep down I felt, in spite of sorrow and bitter tears: "It is right like this. Her life was over. There was nothing pleasant in store for her—it was a release from heavy pain. I must be thankful that she passed away unconsciously like this."

I am also most thankful to our doctor, Dr. Zifferer, who stood by my mother and all of us in those hours with such kindly solicitude.

I dared not abandon myself to my grief as my heart would have wished; there was no understudy for Arabella—the singer who had done the Dresden *première* was not free, nor could she possibly have taken my place without a rehearsal in the completely different production—*Arabella* was the most important *première* of the year; critics and musicians had come to Vienna from everywhere; the house was sold out. . . .

So I sang at the *première.* . . .

There were moments when I forgot the sorrow I bore, whose magnitude only those can realize who have been attached to their mothers as I was to mine. . . .

I was no longer Lotte Lehmann, a daughter bowed down with grief. I was Arabella . . . immeasurable boon of being an artist!

Only when I got back home did I break down and weep.

213

The very next day after we had laid our beloved mother in her grave, I left Vienna. I had a European concert tour to fulfill, and I knew that only concentrated work would help me to get over my grief. This time I did not take my maid Resi as usual; instead I took Mama's nurse Marie whom I had, of course, immediately taken into my service. She was absolutely broken down with grief, and the long journey and a completely different life were the best way for her to get over it.

We celebrated Christmas at home in quiet remembrance of our parents.

"At home"—the meaning of the word is almost lost for me. "Home" was wherever my parents lived—they were the roots, the home-earth. Now the whole world is my "home" . . . a bright, boundless world. . . .

I sometimes get homesick when, in the middle of the hubbub of New York, I think of my quiet little country house at Hinterbrühl where my parents lived and which, for a few weeks in the year, is my refuge. Or when in a restaurant they suddenly play a Viennese song between jazz numbers. . . . Or when I think of the wonderful Vienna Opera where I still feel at home—in spite of the many new faces. . . .

Or when I am on a German ship and hear a steward talking the Hamburg dialect—and suddenly Sylt rises up before me, and Hiddensee. . . . But I also find myself feeling homesick when I am in Vienna and recall to mind the grandeur of the "sky line" in Central Park—the rows of sky-

214

scrapers in the sunny haze beyond the great expanse of grass, like gigantic towers of Babylon . . . or the enormous Californian eucalyptus trees that always look a little wild and unkempt with their shimmering bark hanging down in long strips and their long, narrow, fluttering leaves like wild strands of hair. . . . Or the graceful pepper trees that always remind me of the touching beauty of our birches, with their delicate light-green foliage and the red pepper fruits. . . . Or the tall mimosa trees weighed down with their heavy load of intoxicating golden fragrance. . . . All those things are somehow a part of me. . . . Where then is my "home"? . . .

CHAPTER
TWENTY-FOUR

UNFORTUNATELY I have no memory for dates. So I can only give a disconnected account of what comes into my mind. Perhaps I even forget very important things—but it is a judgment on me for not being more careful and keeping a diary.

It was during this period that I sang with Furtwängler for the first time, as Eva in a very fine *Meistersinger* performance at the Berlin State Opera, and later I did Sieglinde with him in Paris and Vienna. We got on magnificently together.

Shortly after Christmas 1933 I again went to the United States with my husband.

My husband had made a secret plot with Balogh, my American accompanist; he had engaged the "personal representative" for me that I had so fervently rejected. . . . Shortly before our arrival he told me that my manager Coppicus had got a secretary specially for me who in future would be my personal representative. I thought that was very nice of Coppicus and thanked him, when he met us at the docks, for taking so much trouble. He had been let into the secret and received my thanks with a rather embarrassed smile.

216

Previously, at the quarantine station, the lady with the grand-sounding title had come on board. I thought she was charming, although I was a little scared of her tremendous business capabilities. Later Constance confessed that she had been just as frightened of me, as it had been impressed on her that she mustn't make too much publicity, but must go nicely and cautiously with this European who was so devoid of understanding. . . .

So that was Constance Hope and she really needs a chapter to herself! I call her "the cleverest girl in America." . . . She is uncannily clever and able. She is a "businesswoman" and at the same time a genuine enthusiast. An uncommon mixture. In the American style, she is matter-of-fact to her fingertips with a passion for romance in her soul. Moreover, she is young and pretty. She is very fond of me but that does not prevent her from dragging me quite relentlessly through all the hells of publicity if she thinks it is necessary. Unfortunately I can seldom resist her and generally give in after a preliminary show of violent resistance, even submitting to being interviewed at the most inopportune moments when I am dead tired . . . or having some photograph taken whose deep import has not been entirely revealed to me. At a flower show, for instance, near a cactus plant which has interested me least in the whole place—or at a dog show beside a mastiff, when my heart is drawn to the sweet little Pomeranians or the stiff-legged, cheeky rough-haired terriers . . . with children, *seemingly* singing something to them . . . with countless parcels, coming home from "shopping." . . . It is in this way that I am brought to the attention of the great American public—but it is necessary, I admit it. Not that someone like Constance can make one a success, but she can cultivate one's success. She can tell the newspapers about it, and all those little "stories" which I often find so terribly primitive, have their own public. . . . I have long ceased to be annoyed when in an account of an interview there is something quite different from what I have said. The great public wants to think of its favorites above all as just "human beings," in contra-distinction to a time just past, when they wanted to hear of splendor and glamour and sensational extravagances. That is now the fate of the unfortunate movie star; but a singer, especially a famous singer, they want as uncomplicated and near them as possible, not far removed and veiled in a cloud. Perhaps it contributes a little to the secret of my success, that I can never be anything but simple and natural. . . . The well-known New York journalist and authoress, Marcia Davenport, for instance, after a short interview, wrote an article on me in a weekly paper which annoyed me terribly: she did nothing but give details of my everyday life which seemed entirely unimportant to me. However, wherever I went, reporters spoke of it. People who came to the artists' room for autographs after concerts told me how glad they were that I was such a simple "human being." . . . Later, when Marcia and I had become great friends, we often laughed over that article which had started our acquaintance on such an unjustly jarring note.

218

CHAPTER
TWENTY-FIVE

THE year 1934 brought me a tremendous step forward— I sang for the first time at the Metropolitan Opera House. They could no longer exclude me after my great concert successes. Maria Jeritza had retired from there after an exceptionally magnificent series of fabulous triumphs. . . . But I found other well-known faces there at my debut as Sieglinde. Melchior was my Siegmund; Schorr, Wotan; Kappel, Brünhilde; and Karin Branzell, Fricka. It seemed just like a London performance, so familiar was every member of the cast to me. Bodanzky conducted an inspired performance, and I got on splendidly with him straight away. I have a deep artistic affinity with Lauritz Melchior's unforgettable and unsurpassable Siegmund, just as I believe that he regards me as "his Sieglinde." On that day as always, it was a great joy for us to be united again on the stage as the Walsung pair, on a stage—well did I know it—where the best artists in the world had trod. It had for long been my dream and ambition to sing and to conquer there, and the fulfillment was a pride and joy to me!

Recitals, which now occupy most of the year, took us to Cuba. We flew from Miami to Havana in a few hours by a giant plane that held thirty-six passengers. The bright southern land lay in January in the blazing heat of the sun. My recitals which took place in the early part of the afternoon, were torture in the heat, but this was richly compensated for by the great enthusiasm of the audience, whose hunger and appreciation for music was far beyond all expectations. After the recital, Balogh and I looked at each other and laughed; we looked as if we had just come out of a bath. My carefully curled hair was transformed into an "Eton crop," and Balogh's collar lay like a wet rag round his neck. The shower in the hotel was the best moment in the day. . . . Of course we swam every day in the sea, although it was behind a net that was put up to keep off greedy sharks. . . . At night we slept under mosquito nets with bloodthirsty mosquitoes zooming all round—and our bedroom in the Grande Hotel Nazionale had still a big shell hole in the wall from the revolution a few days previously. . . . On the second morning I was awakened by a terrific volley of shots. "Revolution!" was my first thought, and I sounded the alarm. . . . The grinning black servant reassured me— they were only shooting to celebrate the election of a new president. The Cubans shoot on any provocation whatso. ever. . . . In the evening we came back to our hotel earlier than we had intended, for we could scarcely bear the tumult of rejoicing in the street: the whole of Havana seemed to have gone mad. Ear-splitting shrieks, whistles and shots were united in an unbearably strident symphony.

It is very hard not to become a hopeless lounger in Havana. . . . You cannot go to bed those warm, exciting nights—it is as if there were champagne in the air. You want to drift aimlessly along in the crowd of strolling loiterers, or sit outside the big café opposite the "Capitol," brightly lit up with extravagant illuminations, and listen to the Cuban Women's Band playing their wild rhythms and strange melodies. . . . Beggars crowd round your table. It has gone round that "those Americans will give you something" (any foreigner is an American to them). . . . So there they stand, negroes and Cubans, children and gray-beards. . . . There was one sweet little rascal of about six, perfectly beautiful with his yellow-pale dirty little face, big black eyes and wild glossy hair. He was clad in picturesque rags. He noticed that I was taken with him, and then began a regular pantomime; after desperate pleading he tried coaxing smiles, then he danced the Rumba looking roguishly at me out of the corners of his eyes—and always there was his grubby little hand stretched out begging: "Missa, one cent." . . . Those are the first words they learn, the little monkeys: "Mister, one cent."

The delightful members of the Austrian colony who took charge of us in the most kind way during our stay in Havana constantly warned us against giving so much. And finally we were compelled literally to flee from the importunate band

221

of children who kept screaming in chorus: "Missa, one cent. . . ." Our kindly guide, Herr von Novotny, took us by car across country, past sugar plantations and negro huts of incredible wretchedness. But my sympathy for them was perhaps really quite out of place—they want nothing more of life; they eat sugar cane, fruit which drops into their mouth, so to speak, fish, which is ridiculously cheap, and are immoderately lazy. They lie about in the sun until they are hungry, and then work just enough to get a few cents for fish and bread, but no more—Heaven forbid! I took a great many shots of them and they came running up readily, men, women and children—"Missa, one cent. . . ."

I hope it is all really as we were told. For otherwise it would be frightful to have to live in such bitter poverty in the midst of such reckless profusion of nature. . . .

We were lucky enough to have another party with our new friends of the Austrian colony before we left; the table was decorated with Austrian and Cuban flags, I was declared an honorary member, and we reveled in Baccardi-cocktails, champagne, fish and wonderful pineapple that taste quite different there from the ones we get in Europe or any country where they have to be transported. Transport is probably very bad for them, for, freshly plucked, they have a quite indescribable aroma.

As we flew back, the last thing we saw was the Austrian flag waving us farewell from the airport. . . . I experienced an unforgettable sunset on this flight: shortly before we came

222

to Miami, the sea lay below us like heavy molten silver. Slowly delicate colors descended like veils, colors of such unreal beauty as can only exist in a painter's dreams. But a painter would have been mute and breathless before this unreal reality. . . .

Our huge white plane floated through the evening glow toward the fairyland of Florida. . . . I only spent a few hours on Miami beach, sitting in a garden under incredibly lofty palms, surrounded by flowers in extravagant profusion, shining glowworms and silver night-moths—and listening to the sound of the lazy dreaming waves as they rolled to the shore. . . . It was difficult to tear oneself away from this southern Paradise and go back to the cold of winter and ice and snow. My next concert was in Milwaukee—in the Middle West. The train was delayed on account of snowdrifts, and the heating in the carriages froze. . . . Oh Florida—oh Havana!

CHAPTER
TWENTY-SIX

IN FEBRUARY, 1934, I sang for the first time with Arturo Toscanini. He had consented to conduct at the General Motors hour on the radio, and I was chosen as his soloist.

The radio in America is run on quite a different system from ours in Europe. It is commercialized, but on account of the tremendous competition, it offers much more than a state system ever could. The most famous orchestras with their eminent conductors and world-stars as soloists are presented to the public and radio-listening does not cost them a cent. Everything is run on a basis of "advertisement." Thus a firm buys an hour on the radio and in the course of that time has a few minutes' opportunity of extolling its goods. The more interesting the program, the surer they are of a large audience. Enormous fees are paid and there is terrific competition to have the best hour possible. Motor firms, gramophone manufacturers, industries of all kinds have their radio hours. I sing every year in the General Motors and also in the Ford hour, and it does not matter that they are in a way rival concerns. . . . Practically every make of cigarettes has its radio hour. And one can calculate how much a firm of any kind is willing to spend by the fact, for instance, that throughout the whole season the Saturday afternoon performance of the Metropolitan Opera is always transmitted. And when they can hear a Flagstad and a Melchior sing, people will turn on their radio everywhere—in the towns and the farthest outposts. . . . One can sing in the most extraordinary hours—to advertise cheese (this is no joke!) or toothpaste or stores. . . . One soon gets used to thinking it not funny that between two symphonies there should be talks on motor tires. . . . Moreover America has every reason to be very grateful to radio, for in this way the best music is circulated through the entire land by the most distinguished exponents. I find a noticeable increase in musical interest and appreciation wherever I go, and I believe that the radio has had an eminently educative effect.

The General Motors hour in February, 1934, was a double *première;* Toscanini was conducting at a commercial hour for the first time, and I was singing for him for the first time. I had been tremendously impressed by him in his concert with the Philharmonic I had heard shortly before. At the piano rehearsal I trembled so much that I could scarcely sing my program, which consisted of the "Fidelio" aria, and the "Halls of Song" aria from *Tannhäuser.* But the object of my terror seemed so mild and friendly that my fears vanished and I sang with my usual freedom. Later I had the privilege of singing under his baton on various occasions. I was sub-

225

jugated to his fanatical will like everybody else who comes under the spell of that marvelous personality. I saw how he suffered when something was not done exactly as he wanted to have it—not from caprice, but from a relentless pursuit of the very highest perfection. He demanded absolute precision and at the same time the most complete spiritual surrender to the music, an ideal that must remain an unattainable ideal for those who do not happen to be gods. . . . This man, god and demon in one form, it would seem, makes the same ruthless demands on himself as he does on everyone who works with him. And so it is always a fearful pleasure to sing under him. . . . It makes me twice as miserable when I am working with him and something doesn't go as I want it, for, added to the depression every sincere artist feels inwardly when he knows "that wasn't as perfect then as it should have been," is the sorrow of knowing that the Mæstro is depressed . . . for he is unhappy, in the truest sense of the word, at any inadequacy. . . .

It was a long time before I succeeded in completely shaking off the shackles of nervousness.

But heavenly were those hours when, borne on the fiery compelling will of the "great magician" at the desk, I could soar away, opening up and pouring myself out in an ecstasy of song. . . .

At the time of my first concert with him I was nearly fainting with excitement, and I remember on the way to the broadcasting studio how I envied all the people in the streets, pur-

226

First Concert with Toscanini.

suing their peaceful, bourgeois professions . . . not leading a life like mine, made up of an endless succession of heights and depths, a perpetual struggle, a nerve-racking "rejoicing to high Heaven or being cast down to the depths." . . .

A few days after my concert with Toscanini I sang a few lieder at the Beethoven Association, and just before I went on I said to Balogh: "Oh, I feel so calm. An easy program, a nice appreciative audience, and no Toscanini there to be frightened of. . . ." And—my first glance at my audience fell on the Mæstro. . . . My voice and my breath completely deserted me. . . .

Later I often had the honor of knowing that he was present at performances and concerts where I was singing. And it always acted as a great stimulus to me, giving me greater concentration and inspiring in me an even greater devotion to my artistic work.

Only those who are eternally dissatisfied with themselves and their achievements can understand this urge to perfection. What a comfortable and peaceful existence it must be to wander on, with no inner conflict, over a wide plain whose horizon is darkened by no threatening cloud nor bounded by any steep mountain. . . . But such people miss those breathless moments of ecstasy when one looks down on the cloud-hung valley from the vanquished mountain top. . . . Those who love fighting know the proud satisfaction of conquering— and dream of new battles. . . .

In spring of 1934 I sang Tatiana in Tschaikowsky's *Eugen*

227

Onegin in Vienna under Bruno Walter, and marveled anew at Walter's wonderful eye for the scenic. Working with him is a pure joy to me, feeling that loving absorption in his work, and his exhaustive penetration of each part: he never gets lost in externals, but draws its spiritual content from the music and the words as if from a magic well. . . .

In August, Salzburg experienced the proud joy of reckoning Toscanini as one of its own for the first time during the Festival: he conducted two Philharmonic concerts in one of which I was soloist. It was an immensely valuable asset to have succeeded in interesting the great Mæstro in the Festival: the two men who deserve the credit are Baron Puthon and Dr. Kerber who head the Festival committee, and they may well be proud. Toscanini was greatly taken with the charm of Salzburg—the festival atmosphere of the old Mozartian town and the immense effort at all costs to help to build up a shrine consecrated by tradition. So he left Salzburg with the promise that the following year he would conduct *Fidelio* and *Falstaff*, which would certainly introduce a new note in this Festival hitherto almost exclusively devoted to German works. But the *Falstaff* performance was very near to the Mæstro's heart, and haste was made to fulfill his wishes, very much to the benefit of the Festival!

In Autumn, Professor Burghauser, the very active president of the Vienna Philharmonic, succeeded in luring Toscanini back to Vienna to conduct an orchestral concert. And I received a great distinction: the Philharmonic, to whom I am bound by the ties of friendship and artistic affinity, presented me with their Ring of Honour at a concert rehearsal under Weingartner. I was quite unprepared for it and great were my pride and joy. I thanked them with much emotion and then went on to say: "One gives a ring to one's bride in token of inseparable union. Now you have given me the betrothal ring, and have made me, so to speak, the bride of the Philharmonic. . . . At the betrothal there ought to be a kiss. . . . But I can't possibly kiss the whole Philharmonic—but please all of you accept this kiss I give your president."

And amid general applause I embraced Burghauser.

I was the first woman to receive this Ring of Honour, and I am very proud of the fact. Elisabeth Schumann was then similarly honored. For many years I have been very great friends with her and have a sincere admiration for her exquisite artistry. Her fine feeling for style, her immaculate technique, and the crystal clearness of her tone have made her a mæstra of lieder-singing and an incomparable Mozart exponent. Her voice is a hovering of silvery chimes, a soothing, stilly blessing. There is no straining after effect, nothing false: it is pure and noble art. The accents of passion and fervent surrender are foreign to her—they would destroy the framework of this delicate filagree art.

Throughout the world there are connoisseurs of music. They are Elisabeth Schumann's public, in Europe as in America.

During the winter season, which I spent "over there" as I

229

usually do now, Krauss left the Vienna State Opera and transferred himself and his following to Berlin. Felix von Weingartner came to the rescue—and he had the fairly thankless task of having to build up a new company, so to speak, for Krauss had enticed away all his favorite mainstays in the company to the Berlin Opera. . . . Dr. Kerber, the tried and trusty conductor of the Salzburg Festival was made deputy conductor to Weingartner.

CHAPTER
TWENTY-SEVEN

I NOW live abroad a great deal. But whenever I go back to Vienna, I find the love and friendship of my Opera and my public waiting me. I must be grateful that I am so much appreciated and that they don't think too badly of my apparent unfaithfulness to the institution to which I owe my success. . . . It was a moving and happy moment when our honored chancellor, Dr. von Schuschnigg, presented me with the Golden Cross of Austria. I wear this decoration with pride—although no outward sign was needed to bear witness to my inner allegiance to Vienna.

At Salzburg, in the Festival month of August, 1935, Toscanini gave us his magnificent *Fidelio* and his virtuosic *Falstaff*. I had only known the Mæstro as a concert-conductor and now experienced the two-fold sensation of finding in the man who, in concerts, is enthroned on cloudy heights, the artist who belongs to the theater to his fingertips. . . . The fanatical frenzy of this extraordinary personality compels all who work under him to give their utmost. He won't stand any slackness or "routine work." Every rehearsal is like the actual performance to him, and every performance is a "festival performance" . . . far removed from the commonplace which doesn't seem to exist for him. . . . He hardly speaks any German but understands every word, and, although an Italian, he has such a fine ear for German pronunciation that he constantly corrects words if the diction is not clear enough for him. . . . It amazed me to find how a pure musician like him works from the dramatic text. A vividly acted performance is as important to him as a complete realization of the music. Through his sharp eyeglass he notices everything, nothing escapes that keen relentless eye. He does not seem to like wearing pince-nez—he folds them up into a monocle and there he sits, as terrifying and unapproachable as a vengeful god. . . . Everyone trembles before his wrath which is boundless—bursting forth from his boundless fanaticism like a stream of lava from the never-extinguished fires of a crater. . . . One "bravo" from him, or a smile of satisfied acquiescence—and everyone breathes again. . . .

His *Fidelio*—impregnated with intense tragedy—was a tremendous and sensational success. He himself hates anything "sensational"—and yet he is sensational in spite of himself. People crowd round him although he makes every effort to avoid them, he is pursued and persecuted by curiosity wherever he goes. When his fine big Cadillac draws up outside the Opera House, photographers, whom he particularly detests, are waiting for him, autograph-hunters fall on him and are furiously rebuffed. He arrives at the rehearsal,

232

irritated and angry, takes no notice of anyone and stands malevolently waiting by the piano. . . . The world he wants to know nothing of has made him furious, but soon he is under the spell of the music, and in the attaining of his wishes his anger is transformed to beaming smiles. . . . Not that one can put too much trust in those smiles—a badly-sung phrase or an uninspired word of dialogue and storms gather in the dark eyes and the convulsively frowning brow. Rehearsals with him were a perpetual "shaking and quaking in anguish and pain. . . ." But what a compensation that *Fidelio* was!

A dark cloud hung over that summer's Festival. Salzburg's great son Richard Mayr was very ill—and his closest friends suspected that it was hopeless. I visited him as often as my time permitted, and with grief and anguish I watched that dear, noble person, that wonderful artist fading away. Grief brings people closer together than shared joys; my admiration for him grew into a warm friendship, and a feeling of great love and sympathy drew me to his wife who was undergoing all the torments of impotent sorrow, and whose faithful and devoted self-sacrifice kept her by the agonized side of her dying husband. In Richard Mayr, Vienna and Salzburg in particular lost something quite unique. His name is engraved in letters of gold in the annals of the Vienna Opera.

In Autumn, 1935, I took my two maids Resi and Marie to New York with me. We rented a private apartment, for I did really miss "my own home," and hoped in this way to create a substitute for the Viennese home I had left behind me.

My good old Maltese dog Pizzi had died at the age of fifteen, and so our little chocolate-brown Pom Mohrle, whom we had inherited from my mother, accompanied us on his first voyage across the wide ocean all by himself. In Chicago a dear friend of mine gave me a charming and very valuable Pomeranian with a blond coat and cheeky little fox-face and cunning black eyes. It came straight from a kennel, was very cowed, and the first few days crawled about on his belly in such distress that we thought he must be crippled. . . . Later when he had "thawed," he developed into the most terrible little yapper and was the most temperamental little devil we ever had. . . . The debut he made was certainly bewildering enough for poor Jimmy. I called him that because as an "American citizen" he had to have a real American name. I was singing the Marschallin on the second day at a Civic Opera performance. Marie was standing listening in the wings with Jimmy in her arms. We couldn't possibly leave him alone at the hotel, so he just had to come along to the Opera. . . . Now in the first act of *Rosenkavalier,* a vendor of animals appears at the Marschallin's levee, praising his wares with the words: "Housedogs small, house-trained and all" (incidentally this was a gross exaggeration where my Jimmy was concerned). By the merest chance there was no dog there that evening. The producer saw the timid little animal in Marie's arms, cried: "Oh that's really splendid" . . . and

234

took it from her in spite of her violent protests. And so, seated at the Marschallin's dressing table I saw with increasing alarm the animal-vendor with Jimmy, paralyzed with fear, and, in the wings, desperate gesticulations from Marie. . . . Jimmy's debut was a complete success; indeed, I was rather offended that none of the critics mentioned his dignified demeanor. . . . At Buffalo he had another exciting experience: we went back to look at the Niagara Falls which, freed from ice and snow, now plunged down with full overwhelming force in terrifying mass and deafening thunder. Under one part of the falls a gallery has been built out, and we decided to walk along it; it is a passage along the cliffs roofed over with stones and boardings, and it is a creepy sensation to know that above you the wide arcs of the water are plunging down with murderous force. . . . You are given a complete outfit before you enter this passage under the falls—huge gum boots, oilskins and watertight hoods. With Jimmy under my arm I appeared in the cloakroom to be "arrayed for Niagara." Jimmy was supposed to wait for us with the cloakroom attendant, but he set up such a heart-rending yowling that I decided to take him along. So he was given a little oilskin with a diminutive hood and sat like a child on my arm, with his little fox-face peering anxiously out of the hood—what a pity there is no snapshot of us both in existence! . . . Mohrle had stayed behind in New York to guard the flat with Resi, so he missed this exciting journey, which Jimmy perhaps often thought of with longing in the

235

peace of the kennel. . . . Gradually they both became blasé globe-trotters, unimpressed even by long stretches like the one from New York to San Francisco. . . .

Constant variety has now become second nature with me; like a bright flimmering kaleidoscope the revolving colors rotate before my eyes for so long that at last they all seem to be fused into one single color. . . . And when I try now to recollect details of my American tours, East and West and North and South seem merged in one. . . .

There was a negro church at Atlanta in south Georgia with with extraordinary ecstatic ancient negro spirituals . . . the choir were in white robes that made their dark faces stand out strangely. . . . The priest had heard that I was attending the service and greeted me with an address and asked me what songs I would like to hear. I chose that beautiful one, "Going Home," and it moved me to tears.

We frequently spend Christmas at Atlantic City. . . . In summer this ocean resort near Philadelphia is said to be unbearably overcrowded. In winter I like being there for a day or two. Walks along the broad promenade—about eight miles long—and morning swims in the hotel sea-water pool work wonders.

New York is always my home from home. Evenings at the Metropolitan alternate with recitals, and I sing in opera almost everywhere in the country where opera is given—at San Francisco, Philadelphia, Cleveland, Boston. . . . But I do far more concerts.

236

CHAPTER
TWENTY-EIGHT

LAST summer Toscanini, in addition to *Fidelio* and *Falstaff* gave us *Meistersinger* at Salzburg. Free from all ponderousness or sentimentality, he made it a sparkling comedy—breath-taking from beginning to end. Dr. Herbert Graf, a young man of great talent, did the magnificent *décor*. We were all greatly impressed at the dress rehearsal—not that the previous performances were any less fine—but the other rehearsals had been of single acts only, so it was the first time we experienced the work under him as a complete whole. For me it was an unforgettable day—one of life's precious gifts.

We had rented a charming house at St. Gilgen on Lake Wolfgang. Unfortunately it was a rather rainy summer, so we did not have very much of the charming lake, a gem of Austrian scenery. Taking part in a peasants' fete was a real joy for us; every year the Herma Schuschnigg fund provides a magnificent wedding for the poorest couple belonging to a family of long standing in some Austrian district: they get money, household equipment, presents for the wedding guests—and no less a person than the Chancellor himself and his minister Pernter are the witnesses. The bequest is in memory of the wife of our honored Chancellor who was so tragically taken from her husband in the prime of her life. Last summer the choice fell on a bridal couple from St. Gilgen. It was really an enchanting festival, and the sun, which had so often hidden behind rain clouds, shone brilliantly down on this lovely day. From the whole district around came the various guilds in their magnificent old peasant costumes, costly and striking: old damask silks, delicate scarves in shimmering colors, magnificent gold chains that shone and glittered in the sun—it was like a scene from a play with the background of that lovely charming landscape. The Archbishop of Salzburg himself married the young pair who stood, quite dazed at being the recipients of so much honor, suddenly loaded by a benevolent fate with gifts beyond their wildest dreams. . . . The little old church where the wedding took place was crowded—from far and near a stream of guests, augmented by visitors to the Salzburg Festival, came pouring up to see this eventful wedding take place. Mæstro Toscanini and his family also attended the festivities, and he got on so well and was so pleased with all the merriment and so delighted with the marvelous old peasant costumes and customs that I have never seen him so gay. After the feast autograph-hunters crowded round us, and this man who always sternly refused to comply with those requests—which often became a real nuisance—patiently

—Sydney *Morning Herald* and Sydney *Mail*

Arrival in Sydney.

wrote hundreds of autographs until I finally rescued him and carried him off with his family to have tea at my lovely peaceful country house. He even bore without a protest the many cameras turned on him—and that is saying a great deal. I am sometimes afraid that all that boisterous and frequently unrestrained curiosity and enthusiasm with which the crowd pursues him may set him against our dear Salzburg for which he has such a great affection—how great one can see by the touching determination with which he adheres to his plan of helping to develop the Salzburg Festival House. For there is still a great deal to be done there. Originally the performances were conceived on a much smaller scale, but every year the great world comes in increasing numbers to the little Mozart town. Sophisticated "peasant girls" in genuine peasant costumes, elegant men in Salzburg leather shorts and green Tyrolean jackets crowd the narrow streets and make bright waves of color on the bridge, festively resplendent with its decorations of gay flags. In the evenings the sight of huge magnificent cars from every country rolling up is already a commonplace event. Everywhere you hear a Babylonian medley of tongues. . . . People are blissfully happy if they see Max Reinhardt going by—or Bruno Walter—or the Mæstro. . . . In the Café Bazar, world celebrities rub shoulders with wealthy globe-trotters—and even Marlene Dietrich scarcely attracts any special attention—so great is the choice of "notabilities." . . . But the person who was proudest of his popularity was my chauffeur Fritz, when his picture appeared one day in the papers with Toscanini's Emilio, and the inscription: "Two other notabilities." . . .

Felix von Weingartner resigned his post as director of the State Opera but stayed on with us as conductor. Dr. Kerber was appointed director and Bruno Walter artistic adviser. May the wonderful Vienna Opera be destined to have a new period of brilliance under those men!

In autumn I sang only for a few evenings in Vienna and had very soon to leave Europe again. In San Francisco we participated in the opening of the Bay Bridge which connects San Francisco, Oakland and Berkeley in a series of majestic arches over 22,000 feet long. The bridge is a triumph of technique, technique which here has become pure, sublime beauty.

I believe that only a person entirely lacking in imagination can fail to feel the romance of such perfection of technique. . . . When you stand for instance in the wide lobby of the 102nd story of the Empire State Building in the evening with New York at your feet—a world of light, the giant skyscrapers like towers built by children's hands, the houses like beehives broken up into rectangular patterns of light, the glittering line of Broadway with the shimmering cloud of light over it—who could feel this town as anything else than a fairy kingdom? It always fills me with the wonder of a child who opens a picture book in the belief that he will constantly find new marvels there. . . .

240

From San Francisco we made a glorious excursion to the Muir Woods, a primeval forest whose silence tells of thousands of years, and whose lofty trees stand grave and weighty as pillars in a cathdral. . . . The wood is petrified, the roots and the trunks will endure to eternity, but in the twigs there still runs the sap of ever-recurring new life. . . . We did not dare to speak out loud in the solemn stillness around us . . . until the garish light of day brought us back from this cathedral of dreams into the noisy rush of reality again.

Detroit—center of the motor industry! We were shown over the Ford works and saw how cars are made right from the beginning. We followed the process until the finished article stood before us all ready to start. . . . It seemed quite surprising that the chauffeur wasn't sent up on a feed-belt as well. . . .

The amazing functional activity of this enormous factory town reminded me a little of the precise mechanism of my tours. . . . One runs a certain risk of becoming mechanized oneself in this wholesale process. . . . But the living stream flows strong and steady between its confining banks, and the eternal melody of its waters will never be mute. . . .

And so my song is constantly renewed at the sacred flame. . . .

I cannot imagine that the day will come when I get tired of my profession. . . . Sometimes, when from my lovely flat near the park I hear the ocean liners in the docks shrieking like homesick beasts and know that they come from Europe,

241

I long for the so much more peaceful life of Vienna. Yet I know that I could not stand it permanently—my whole being is in the grip of the terrific tempo of our time. There is a disquiet in my veins that will not let me rest. . . .

Nor can I rest from my pursuit of perfection.

It is no coincidence, nor is it the outcome of the routine of international tours, that I penetrate ever more into the purer and more heavenly kingdom of lieder-singing: it is my longing for artistic perfection that has led me thither. I have sung in opera for many years—and I certainly do not want to end my operatic career. There are still fine and glorious tasks before me—a new summer Festival at Salzburg with *Fidelio* under Toscanini, the Marschallin under that splendid conductor Knappertsbusch, the recital with Bruno Walter, the Elisabeth under the Mæstro . . . The Metropolitan is asking for me again and I love singing there.

But I don't want to be permanently tied to any opera house.

A new generation has grown up—and many of my successors will go the way I have been privileged to go. I wish it from the depths of my heart, for I know how blessed it is to achieve an end. . . .

And yet I am far from putting finis to this book, the writing of which has given me such immense pleasure; I still see heights before me, starry peaks. . . . I have so much to say to the world—so much to give. . . .

Songs keep pouring in as if from inexhaustible springs.

To master them, to give my soul to them—what finer task is there in life?

When I stand before a new audience, I know that it is not only my own name that I must do credit to, but also the two opera houses to which I belong—the Vienna Opera and the New York Metropolitan. I had my artistic education in Vienna. It is my true "home," even though the great wide world has become my dwelling place. . . . It is lovely to know that somewhere in the glittering vortex of my life is my "home." Of course there are many new faces at the old Opera House when I go back every year, and I feel the passage of time twice as strongly when I come home and always find something new and strange. . . . It would perhaps make me sad if I didn't feel that I myself were receding farther and farther from this world of the stage. Soon it will be only "festival performances" and I shall be only a guest. . . .

I will not end on a note that sounds like estrangement, or with a thought that might seem like resignation; I have collected past and present into a bright nosegay. Now I will continue along the gleaming path of the future. . . . It calls me to pluck a new nosegay, fresh and blooming. Perhaps it will be even lovelier than anything that has gone before.

This shall be my hope—and my belief.

THE END

INDEX

INDEX

Aïda, 110
Altona, 105, 116
Alwin, Carl, 157, 180
Arabella, 212, 213
Ariadne, 141-142, 180, 191
Arndt, 77
Athens, 181

Bachur, Councilor, 91, 104, 107, 109
Bahia Blanca, 152
Bake, Professor, 63, 64
Balogh, Ernö, 200, 202-203, 216, 220
Bartels, Elise, 50
Barthou, 179
Beecham, Sir Thomas, 123, 171
Berlin, 22-23, 177
Berlin Court Opera, 112, 113
Berlin State Opera, 157, 216
Blois, Eustace, 156, 171
Bodanzky, 219
Bohnen, 123
Branzell, Karin, 219
Braun, Carl, 150
Brecher, Gustav, 92, 96-99, 109-110, 124
Brossement, Frau Professor, 115
Brunswick, Duchess of, 149
Bucharest, 88
Buenos Aires, 151-152
Burghauser, Professor, 228, 229
Bürs, 121, 135
Busch, Fritz, 158

California, 205
Canada, 210
Carl, Emperor, 144
Caruso, Enrico, 106-109
Charlottenburg Opera, 157
Chicago, 182, 185-186, 187-188

Chicago Civic Opera, 182, 183, 186, 198
Clemenceau, Paul, 179
Cologne, 123
Constantinople, 146
Coppicus, 188, 195, 198, 216
Covent Garden, 124, 156, 167, 169, 171
Cuba, 220-221
Culp, Julia, 61
Cumberland, Duke of, 148

Dahn, 79, 88
D'Albert, 135, 136
Davenport, Marcia, 218
Destinn, 36
Detroit, 241
Don Gil von den grünen Hosen, 180
Dresden, 157, 158, 212, 213
Drill-Orridge, Theo, 117, 119, 120, 121, 135

Elizza, Elise, 115, 141
Erhardt, Dr., 171
Eugen Onegin, 227-228
Evangelimann, 111, 118

Falstaff, 228, 231, 237
Farrar, Geraldine, 198
Ferdinand und Luise, 180
Fidelio, 161-163, 169, 172, 179, 228, 231, 232-233, 237, 242
Figaro, 65, 171
Fledermaus, 169
Fleischer-Edel, Katharina, 105, 108, 115, 116, 119
Foll, Ferdinand, 152, 167-168
Francillo-Kauffman, Hedwig, 114
Franz Joseph I, 144

247

Frau ohne Schatten, 148, 182
Freischütz, 63, 77, 96, 124, 125, 140
Furtwängler, 216

Gerster, Etelka, 58-60, 71
Grand Canyon, 206
Gregor, 121, 139-140, 148
Grüning, 36
Günther, Karl, 118, 121
Gutheil-Schoder, Marie, 141-142, 144

Habig, Eduard, 183
Hamburg, 89, 90, 122, 132-133
Hamburg Municipal Theater, 89, 102, 118, 132-133, 141
Harder, 87, 112
Harmans, 98
Havana, 220-223
Heger, Robert, 171
Heimchen am Herd, 104
Hensel, Heinrich, 118
Herriot, 179
Hiddensee, 56, 164-165
Hiedler, 36
Hempel, Frieda, 123
Hindenburg, 165
Hinterbrühl, 155, 175, 198, 211, 214
Hollywood, 207-208
Hope, Constance, 218-219

Intermezzo, 157, 159, 180
Iphigénie, 121
Ivogün, Maria, 156

Jelenko, 99, 100-102, 107-108, 122-123
Jerger, 180
Jeritza, Maria, 142, 143, 146, 148, 180, 219
Jordan, Helene, 45, 49, 57
Jüdin, Die, 134

Kalisch, Betty, 60
Kalter, Sabine, 119
Kappel, 219

Kaszowska, Felicia, 115, 161
Kerber, Dr., 230, 240
Kittel, Hermina, 141
Kirchhoff, 150
Kiurina, Berta, 141
Klemperer, Otto, 92, 111, 112, 116, 117, 207
Knappertsbusch, 242
Krauss, Clemens, 190, 193, 212, 230
Kuhreigen, 180
Kurz, Selma, 141, 142, 146

Lamperti, 115
Landau, Felix, 93
Lehmann, Fritz, 2-5, 7, 10, 13, 17-19, 25, 26-29, 34, 46, 47, 51, 52, 59, 69-70, 85, 90, 165, 199
Leider, Frieda, 156, 183
Lichtenstein, Eduard, 105
Lion, 144-145
Loewenfeld, Dr. Hans, 110-111, 113, 116, 122-123, 134-136
Loewengard, Max, 111, 113
Lohengrin, 36, 63, 96, 180
Lohfing, Max, 105-106
London, 123-124, 156, 169
Los Angeles, 207, 208
Ludwig II, 73

Maikl, Georg, 141
Mallinger, Mathilde, 71-74, 76-80, 91
Manuel, King, of Portugal, 170-171
Marak, Otto, 119
Marcelle, Lucille, 110
Marchesi, 58, 61
Mascagni, 150
Mayr, Richard, 128, 131, 141, 143, 146, 148, 156, 172, 233
Meistersinger, 77, 96, 109, 152, 216, 237
Melchior, Lauritz, 156, 219
Merry Wives, 98, 101
Metropolitan Opera, 182, 219, 225, 242, 243
Metzger-Lattermann, Ottilie, 119

Meyrowitz, Selmar, 121
Miami, 220, 223
Mignon, 36
Milan (Scala), 157
Mocchi, 150
Montevideo, 153

Nemeth, Maria, 161
New York, 183, 195-198, 202, 210,
214, 233, 240, 243
Niagara Falls, 210, 235
Nikisch, Arthur, 103

Oestvig, Aagard, 143, 148
Olszewska, Maria, 156, 169, 180, 183
Onegin, Sigrid, 156
Orpheus, 106

Paalen, Bella, 141, 143
Painlévé, 179
Paris, 163, 167, 178, 196
Paris Grand Opera, 167
Parsifal, 119
Pennarini, 116
Petschnikoff, Lily, 207-208
Pfitzner, Hans, 124
Piccaver, Alfred, 141, 143, 146
Pollak, Egon, 183,186
Puccini, 147
Putlitz, Baron zu, 62-63, 85
Putlitz, Baron Konrad zu, 75-76, 81-
88, 90
Putlitz, Baroness Konrad zu, 75, 76,
79, 81, 82, 83, 85-86
Putlitz, Elisabeth zu, 81, 82
Putlitz, Erika zu, 81, 82-83

Rechberg, Countess Gabi, 180
Reinhardt, Delia, 156
Reinhold, Eva, 58-61, 64-68, 71
Reszke, Jean de, 115
Rheingold, 102
Rienzi, 104
"Ring," The, 171
Riviera, The, 173-174

Rizza, Gilda dalla, 150
Roller, Alfred, 129
Rosenek, Leo, 152, 168
Rosenkavalier, 98, 101, 123, 155, 156,
172, 234

Saldern, Frau von, 62, 86
Salter, Norbert, 120-121, 123
Salzburg, 172, 194, 231, 233, 237-239,
242
Salzburg Festival, 65, 172, 194, 231,
233, 237-239, 242
San Francisco, 240
Santa Barbara, 208
Schadow, Alma, 113, 114
Schalk, Franz, 128-129, 141, 148, 155,
161, 168-169, 173, 176, 177, 190-
193
Scheffler, Anna, 119
Scheidt, Bobby von, 105
Schipper, Emil, 150, 156
Schmedes, Erik, 141, 143, 180
Schnabl-Rossi, Riccardo, 147
Schneiderhan, 190
Schorr, Friedrich, 156, 219
Schulze, Professor Adolf, 41-46, 51,
55, 57
Schubert, Richard, 119
Schumann, Elisabeth, 98, 99, 101, 104,
147, 156, 169, 229
Schuschnigg, Dr. von, 231, 238
Sirota, Leo, 148
Sister Angelica, 147
Slezak, Leo, 141, 143, 146, 178
South America, 150
Stabile, 150
Stockholm, 169
Strauss, Richard, 148, 149, 157-158,
168
Stuttgart, 84-87
Sylt, 165-166

Tannhäuser, 96, 124, 225
Tauber, Richard, 125
Teneriffe, 153

249

Tiedke, Erna, 37-44
Toscanini, Arturo, 157, 225-228, 231, 237-239, 242
Tote Augen, 135, 137
Tote Stadt, 180
Tristan und Isolde, 191-192
Turandot, 161

Valkyrie, 152
Venice, 174-175
Venizelos, 181
Vienna, 115, 128, 137, 138, 177, 243
Vienna Court Opera, 120-123, 129-131, 140, 143-144, 148
Vienna New Conservatoire, 199
Vienna Philharmonic, 129, 151, 229
Vienna State Opera, 169, 190-191-193, 214, 231, 233, 240, 243

Wagner, Frau, 116
Wagner, Richard, 77
Walker, Edyth, 99, 106, 109
Wallenstein, Dr., 162-163
Walter, Bruno, 155-157, 168-171, 176-177, 194, 207, 228, 239, 240, 242
Weidemann, Friedrich, 128, 131, 141, 147
Weidt, Lucie, 141, 146, 148, 180
Weingartner, Felix von, 60, 110, 150, 230, 240
Wildbrunn, Helene, 150, 156
Winnipeg, 210
Winternitz-Dorda, Martha, 119
Wymetal, von, 129, 140, 143, 162

Zoppot, 123, 125, 127